Henri Rousseau

Carnival Evening (Un Soir de Carnival). *1886. Oil, 45 x 34¼ inches. Collection Louis E. Stern.*

Henri Rousseau

By Daniel Catton Rich

"I have been told that my work is not of this century. As you will understand, I cannot now change my manner which I have acquired as the result of obstinate toil . . . . "
Henri Rousseau in a letter to the art critic, André Dupont, 1910.

IN COLLABORATION WITH THE ART INSTITUTE OF CHICAGO

THE MUSEUM OF MODERN ART, NEW YORK

Reprint Edition, 1969   *Published for The Museum of Modern Art by Arno Press*

Contents

Foreword

This study of the life and art of Henri Rousseau was prepared to accompany an exhibition of his work arranged in 1942 by The Art Institute of Chicago and The Museum of Modern Art. Prepared during the war, its selection of paintings reflected the fact that it was impossible to borrow canvases from abroad. It was discovered, however, that in American collections alone were sufficient works by the artist to present a comprehensive view of his development. Though the volume includes a few reproductions of well-known paintings not in the exhibition and though frequent reference is made to pictures not available at that time, its analysis is largely concentrated on works familiar to the public in museums or collections in the United States.

The first painting by Rousseau to enter an American museum was, I believe, The Waterfall in the Birch-Bartlett Collection of the Art Institute, when in 1925 it was included in this pioneer gallery of late nineteenth-century and twentieth-century art. Paintings by Rousseau have been shown in many exhibitions at the Museum of Modern Art, particularly in 1938 when some of his works were featured with other "modern primitives" of Europe and America in Masters of Popular Painting. In fact New York saw the first Rousseau exhibition as early as 1910, arranged shortly after his death by his friend, Max Weber, at "291," Alfred Stieglitz's gallery where so many important modern artists were introduced to America. Since that day many Rousseau canvases have entered our private and public collections, for aside from Germany, where he was quickly appreciated, no country, not even his own, has responded so warmly as the United States to his sincere and unassuming art.

In the preparation of this volume I am greatly indebted to several friends of the artist, especially Max Weber who supplied new biographical material of great importance. From critics and students of his art, I received many helpful suggestions and material. I wish to thank particularly James Johnson Sweeney for permission to reproduce a telling photograph from his book, Plastic Redirections in Twentieth Century Painting (Chicago, 1934), and for sending me, through Henri Pierre Roche, a photostat of Rousseau's touching and characteristic letter to the Mayor of Laval, offering to that city his famous canvas, The Sleeping Gypsy, now in the Museum of Modern Art.

For this second edition, a few corrections and additions of both text and illustration have been made and the bibliography has been brought up to date. The study itself spans the period from 1886, the year of Rousseau's first appearance in the Salon of the Inde-

pendents, to his death in 1910. It particularly emphasizes works done after 1900, not only because our collectors found the exotic subjects of the master more to their taste than his portraits and allegories, but since, in my opinion, it was here that the painter achieved the preponderance of those works which have given him fame. Throughout, the object has been to show him not as a "naive" eccentric but as an artist significant in his own right—one of the great and original painters of his generation. This view, so strikingly different from much written on Rousseau, has been strongly contradicted, especially by essayists who admire the "primitive." It is interesting to note, however, that one effect of the exhibition in Chicago and New York has been to diminish critical faith in this easy explanation of his art and a number of recent writers have seen Rousseau in a more objective, if less sentimental light.

DANIEL CATTON RICH, Diréctor
The Art Institute of Chicago

Key

Oil paintings are on canvas unless otherwise noted.
(Dated) following a date means that the date appears on the picture.
In dimensions, height precedes width.

Brief Chronology

1844 Born May 20 at Laval, Department of Mayenne, France.

1862 Probably went to Mexico as a regimental musician in the French army sent by Napoleon III to aid Maximilian.

1866 Returned to France.

1867 Demobilized. Became a lawyer's clerk, entered the customs (?).

1870 Served in the French army in the Franco-Prussian War.

1871 Employed in a toll station on outskirts of Paris as a minor inspector, a post he retained until 1885.

1880 First dated paintings.

1885 Retired on small pension to become a professional painter. Lived in Plaisance Quarter, Paris. A widower, he remarried.

1886 Began to exhibit at the Salon of the Independents, showing continuously until his death in 1910, with the exception of the years 1899 and 1900. *Carnival Evening*.

1890 Painted *Myself. Portrait-Landscape*. Acquaintance with Gauguin, Redon, Gustave Coquiot, Seurat and Pissarro.

1891 *Storm in the Jungle*, his first use of exotic material.

1892 *The Centenary of Independence* (see sketch, *The Carmagnole*).

1895 Commissioned by Rémy de Gourmont to draw lithograph for *L'Imagier*.

1897 *The Sleeping Gypsy*. (Offered in 1898 to his birthplace, Laval, for two or three hundred francs but refused by the town.)

1901 *An Unpleasant Surprise*. Was living at 2 bis rue Perrel, Paris.

1904 *Scouts Attacked by a Tiger*, return to tropical theme of *Storm in the Jungle*.

1905 *A Wedding in the Country*. Began to exhibit at the Autumn Salon with three pictures, among them the large and important *Hungry Lion* . . .

1906 Met Robert Delaunay, Vlaminck, Picasso, Guillaume Apollinaire et al. Exhibited at the Independents *Liberty Inviting the Artists to Take Part in the 22nd Exhibition by Independent Artists*.

1907 Commissioned by Madame Delaunay to paint *Snake-Charmer*, which when exhibited at the Autumn Salon elicited praise. Acquaintance with Max Weber and Wilhelm Uhde, later to become his biographer. Joseph Brummer sells a few of his works.

1908 Began Saturday *soirées*, attended by artists and intelligentsia of Paris. Picasso and his friends give Rousseau a banquet in Picasso's studio in the rue Ravignan. *The Cart of Père Juniet*.

1909 January 9. Tried for complicity in fraud connected with the Bank of France. Convicted but due to age and obvious innocence in worldly affairs, sentence was remanded.

1910 Unsuccessful love affair with Madame Léonie. Painted *The Dream*. Died, September 4.

1911 Retrospective exhibition, Salon of the Independents. Biography by Uhde appears.

9

Myself. Portrait-Landscape. 1890 (dated). Oil, 57½ x 44¾ inches. Collection The Modern Museum, Prague.

Henri Rousseau

For half a century the art of Henri Rousseau has been obscured by an insistent and almost exclusive belief in its primitivism. Because the artist was self-taught and thereby lacked the studio training of his day, Rousseau was first scorned, then loved for his "naïveté." His enthusiasts allowed him no sources or development. He was simply a "primitive" (as the twentieth century conceived one) and automatically produced "marvelous" and "angelic" works in a vacuum. Though critics glorified the man (hundreds of stories exist to prove his ingenuousness) they tell little of his art. Three decades after Rousseau's death we lack the most significant details of his biography such as confirmation of his years in Mexico, details of his two marriages, and possible early associations with teachers and other artists; we are uncertain about the chronological order of his paintings and nowhere do we find a serious appraisal of his style.

Henri Julien Félix Rousseau was born in Laval, the chief town of the Department of Mayenne in northwestern France, on May 20, 1844. His family was poor, his father a humble dealer in tin ware (*ferblantier*), but his mother, Eléonore Guyard, seems to have descended from a family of some military prominence. Perhaps the chevaliers and colonels on her side of the house determined Henri to seek an army career. Though records are lacking, it is probable that in 1862, at the age of eighteen, he was sent to Mexico in the service of the ill-starred Emperor Maximilian as a musician in a military band. Returning to France in 1866, he was demobilized the next year and became a lawyer's clerk. Soon afterward he may have entered the customs service but in the War of 1870 he was back in the army with the rank of sergeant, saving (so he told afterwards) the town of Dreux "from the horrors of civil war." In 1871 he was given employment in a toll station on the outskirts of Paris, not as a customhouse officer (*douanier*) but as a minor inspector. All this time he had been compelled, as he says himself, "to follow at first another career than that which his artistic taste called him." Around 1885, when about forty, he retired on a tiny pension, determined to become known as a professional artist.

1880–1885

No painting dated before 1880 exists. But Rousseau had probably drawn and painted all his life. He was entirely self-taught, not because he scoffed at instruction (he later founded an "academy" and gave lessons) but because he had been too poor to enroll in an art school. The first little pictures that survive show him working in the amateur tradition of the 'eighties in France. Every self-taught painter starts under some pictorial influence. Rousseau began with memories of anonymous portraits, flower pieces, little romantic landscapes—the whole retarded idiom of folk painting which, especially since 1800, had been

11

practiced all over Europe and the New World. Regardless of period and quality such works bear a family resemblance.[1] Their forms are carefully adjusted to the surface of the painting and to the frame. The picture surface is developed geometrically, with an often inflexible rhythm of lines and spaces. The execution of details is minutely realistic. And because there usually lies at the bottom of such works the need to express a vital emotion, the result is full of expressive content. Figures with eyes gazing straight ahead are frozen in frontal pose. Perspective is centralized. Strong differences of proportion are stressed (tiny figures in a big landscape, an enormous figure against a dwarfed background) and severe contours surround areas of color, often without shadow or weight.

Rousseau's earliest work displays many of the same characteristics. These small formalized landscapes with water mills and bridges and these little portraits fit closely into the folk idiom. True, they have a lucidity of color, a delicate charm in their geometry which set them apart from the rank and file of amateur paintings, but had Rousseau stopped here he would have been only a forgotten figure in a minor tradition. Instead he chose to teach himself more. He now determined to observe the objective world about him with penetrating eyes and to seek counsel from above. As he himself expresses it, he worked "alone with only nature as a teacher and some advice received from Gérôme and Clément."

His choice of Gérôme is enlightening. In the 'eighties the painter of *The Last Prayer* and *The Two Majesties* was not only an idol of the Salon public, but a powerful professor in the Ecole des Beaux-Arts, where one of his first acts had been an attempt to banish Manet. What he told Rousseau we have no way of knowing. The master always denounced hasty, careless sketches; he encouraged highly idealized and finished painting and at one time stated that the first merit of a canvas lay in its "luminous and alluring color." All this may have been delivered to the struggling painter over forty, just beginning so late in life his chosen career. Rousseau remarks that both Clément and Gérôme encouraged him in his "naïveté." Perhaps they were momentarily stirred out of themselves by a note of engaging freshness, or more likely they were trying to be kind to a man they considered hopeless.

Rousseau's struggle now becomes clear. He dreamed of becoming a great and successful painter but subconsciously he realized the limitations of the folk style. At the same time he stubbornly refused to relinquish its designed stability. His problem was to retain such elements as were intuitively necessary to his art and to transform them into a freer, more individual means of expression. That he was able to accomplish the first step in this solution is eloquently proved by *Carnival Evening* (frontispiece), exhibited in the newly created Salon of the Independents in 1886.

Fortunately for him the new Salon existed. In 1884 a group of painters, rebelling against the dead exclusiveness of the official Salon, organized a yearly showing without prizes or juries, open to all artists. Odilon Redon was a vice-president and the Independents instantly

---

[1] MICHAILOW, NIKOLA. Zur begriffsbestimmung der laienmalerei. Zeitschrift für Kunstgeschichte 4 no5–6: 283–300 1935.

River Scene, Quai d'Auteuil. 1885 (dated). Ink on tan paper, 6½ x 4⅞ inches. Collection Max Weber.

Quai d'Auteuil. 1885 (dated). Ink on tan paper, 6 x 4½ inches. Collection Max Weber.

became the battleground of Pointillism, the first movement to challenge Impressionism, which had been the radical movement of the 'seventies. In the very year that Rousseau made his debut public indignation was running high against Signac, and Seurat's *Sunday Afternoon on the Island of La Grande Jatte* was the scandal of the exhibition.

1886–1891

In *Carnival Evening* the artist poses a problem to which he will return again and again. Two small figures in the foreground are designed against a screen of trees or foliage through which the eye is led, plane by plane, into deep, lighted space. What strikes us at once about this work of 1886 is Rousseau's extraordinary progress in the space of a few years. No longer is his vocabulary confined to a few handed-down forms. The delicate nerve-like branches of the trees are rendered with an authority which springs from a wider experience with nature. Only the sharpest observation could account for the shapes and tones of the cloud bands. And yet all that he takes from the objective world is fastidiously transformed and organized through a system of silhouette and clear light. Inventions of rhythm,

A Rendez-vous in the Forest. 1889. Oil, 36½ x 28¾ inches. Collection Marie Harriman.

correspondences of line abound. To make his vision more compelling, the artist gives every inch of his canvas the same scrupulous and sensitive execution. With a greater liberation of form comes a new sentiment. Rousseau intended *Carnival Evening* as a night poem and in the masquerading figures, the mask at the window, the bare, towering trees and moonlit sky there first appears that note of strangeness so marked in all his imaginative painting.

14

Medieval Castle (Le Château-Fort). *1889 (dated). Oil, 36½ x 38¾ inches. Collection Marie Harriman.*

In the two drawings (page 13) done a year before, Rousseau continues to analyze, with great delicacy, two motifs from nature. Before 1895 Rousseau admits that he made more than "200 drawings in pen and pencil," which must have played an important rôle in the formation of his style.

A Rendez-vous in the Forest (page 14) is full of the same intense observation. The plan of *Carnival Evening* is reversed and the figures, instead of occupying the frontal plane, are seen through a complicated lattice of spring trees. Rousseau ornaments the lower half of the picture with the loving, detailed care of the folk-painter, but when it was finished and each leaf and twig had been woven into the pattern, he may have been dissatisfied with the result. In spite of its highly romantic theme—lovers in eighteenth-century costume meeting in the depths of the forest—it yet lacked much he desired in a picture. And so in its companion, a night piece, *Medieval Castle* (page 15), he boldly designs in larger forms of dark and light, restricting surface elaboration to a few passages in the trees. In place of filigreed planes appears a striking diagonal arrangement of flat areas.

Meanwhile the artist was living with his second wife in the most humble surroundings of the Plaisance quarter in Paris. He did all sorts of small jobs to eke out his pension, such as serving as inspector of sales for a newspaper, writing letters and acting as legal adviser to the poor of the district. His wife opened a little stationery shop where his pictures were always on sale and he painted a certain number of portraits of his neighbors. For a time he taught drawing in a municipal school and was made *Officier de l'Instruction Publique*, wearing the violet button which he proudly displays in his self-portrait of 1890 (page 10). This is a "portrait-landscape," a genre familiar in his work. The model is fitted out with a background appropriate in both sentiment and design. For himself he chose the festive Paris of the *Exposition Universelle* of 1889, complete with Eiffel Tower and balloon. He stands—a much taller figure than in life—holding brush and palette inscribed with "Clémence" and "Joséphine," the names of his two wives. Clearly this is his strongly held vision of himself, a respectable "professor of art" determined to become one of the great painters of his age.

At first the age denied him. Not that his pictures were ignored even when skyed or tucked away in the coldest corners of the Independents where, between the years 1886 and 1890, he showed twenty works. The public found them out and laughed uproariously. Critics poked fun at him. Rousseau did not falter. Industriously he collected his press notices and pasted them into a book. Next to one he noted: "Wrote to the journalist for his insulting article. Made excuses."

But if the public was amused and critics misunderstood, a few artists took a second look at these paintings, which seemed so opposed in style and feeling to the main currents of their day. The decade of the 'eighties saw the start of a major shift in artistic ideals. With the rejection or disciplining of Impressionism interest in the illusion of nature began to slacken. Painters turned back to a more permanent structure, seeking in archaic styles of the past a new way to organize the data of vision. Puvis de Chavannes had feebly indicated one approach. Seurat devised a method to bring order into Impressionism, joining to it the tradition of classical design. And Gauguin went back to the primitive. So it is not surprising to discover Gauguin admiring Rousseau for his "blacks" at a time when black had been fashionably banished from the palette. And about 1888 Odilon Redon and Gustave Co-

16

Storm in the Jungle. 1891 (dated). Oil, 50½ x 63½ inches. Collection Mr. and Mrs. Henry Clifford.

quiot, defender of the Independents, began, according to the latter, "to celebrate Rousseau's genius as a naturalist painter who sometimes attained a beautiful classic style."

Seurat, meanwhile, had sought to energize his stable forms with movement (*Le Chahut*, 1889-90, *The Circus*, 1891); Degas was working with larger rhythms and Toulouse-Lautrec was constantly increasing the activity and flow of his line. All that Rousseau had painted so far was static, fixed and immobile. Such movement as existed came through rhythmic repeat of small elements rather than through any big, inclusive design. But in 1891 he labored hard over a large picture, *Storm in the Jungle* (above). It represents the height of his romanticism and the first use of exotic material. Here he subdued his delight in elaboration of detail to a more general movement of the forms. All is still conceived in planes but the artist now twists and entwines them. Light not only defines but contributes atmosphere to the dramatic theme. The complex color, with contrasts of browns, greens and red, re-

Pont de Grenelle, Paris. 1891–93. Oil, 8 x 29¾ inches. Private collection.

sults in part from the artist's almost literal rendering of plant forms. His chief concession to surface lies in striping the entire canvas with lines of thin rain.

Friends of Rousseau once explained his jungle pictures as memories of his Mexican journey. But today we know they were inspired by trips to the Paris zoo and botanical gardens. In a vaudeville sketch written about this time and entitled *A Visit to the Exposition of 1889* (page 75) one of the ten scenes is, significantly, set in the *Jardin des Plantes*. On his walks around Paris the artist used to pick up leaves and grasses to treasure in his studio. From such sources—transfigured by imagination and design—grew his exotic flora.

1892–1897

During the next few years Rousseau strives constantly to broaden and simplify his style. In such a canvas as *Pont de Grenelle* (above) he sternly limits the number of planes and reduces the color to a few tones. Against the stark areas of snow and the stone bridge, the shapes of figures and lumber-cart are silhouetted with extraordinary force. With complete freedom he combines various perspectives and adjusts space to fill the long, narrow format. Unlike the Impressionists, who preferred the colorful and gay life along the river at La Grenouillère, Chatou or Bougival, Rousseau seldom went far from home for his landscape motifs. He loved the heart of the city with its iron bridges, boats and quays or the quiet

The Carmagnole. 1891–92. Oil, 7½ x 30 inches. Collection Dr. and Mrs. Frank Conroy.

18

Poet's Bouquet (Fleurs de poète). 1890–95. Oil, 15 x 18 inches. Collection William S. Paley.

Sawmill, Outskirts of Paris. 1893–95 (?). Oil, 10 x 18 inches. Collection Mr. and Mrs. Walter S. Brewster.

suburbs where, as in *Sawmill, Outskirts of Paris* (above), he enjoyed painting factory buildings surrounded by trees and foliage. By this time Rousseau is learning not only to bind his forms more strongly into a single geometric unit but to vary his textures. His technique has the same fineness of touch but the touch itself is less uniform or labored.

Color so far had been distinctly subordinate to tone and draughtsmanship. The night pieces of the 'eighties and the detailed color of *Storm in the Jungle* do not prepare us for the bright hues and luminous atmosphere of *The Carmagnole* (page 18). To the Salon of the Independents in 1892 the artist sent as his exhibition piece a large canvas, *The Centenary of Independence. The Carmagnole* is perhaps the first sketch for the big painting. For Rousseau the centenary was a genuinely inspiring event. He wrote an explanation for the catalog: "The people, holding hands, dance round the two Republics, those of 1792 and 1892, to the tune of *Auprès de ma blonde qu'il fait bon, fait bon dormir.*" A year later he addressed a second picture to Liberty ("Oh, Liberty, be forever the guide of those who by their labor wish to contribute to the glory and grandeur of France!") Such sentiments show Rousseau's genuine and simple love of his country but they also indicate his firm belief that as one of the most important artists of the day he must commemorate for the citizens of France the anniversary of their Republic.

Behind the composition may lie a suggestion of some *kermess* by Bruegel or Teniers, but the spirit is gaily French. Notes of color are repeated in the circling figures and in the fluttering banners (all arranged to blow in the same direction), while space is clearly marked

21

off by the reiterated vertical of the flagpoles. When Rousseau came to paint the final version, he changed the format and completely re-designed the whole picture—an indication of how much he continued to respect the relation of a painting to its surface and frame.

But if the artist hoped to win public acclaim by such patriotic subjects he was doomed to disappointment. Indeed, there was even talk on the part of some of the more arbitrary members of the Committee of the Independents of banishing altogether those artists whose work brought nothing but laughter in the annual Salon. Fortunately tolerance won, the painter of *The Carmagnole* being well defended by Toulouse-Lautrec. It is said that Rousseau was in favor of the exclusion, never dreaming for a moment that it was aimed at him.

The still life, *Poet's Bouquet* (page 19), carries on his interest in color and more simplified handling. The background, table top and vase are broadly painted to allow an enriched concentration on the flowers themselves. Not only does he award each blossom and leaf the same prominence, but he tries to communicate the growing sensitive life of flowers even after they are plucked. The ones on the left are significantly set against a blue ground suggesting the sky. Though there are relatively few flowers, Rousseau manages to convey the sense of a complete garden. This ability to make a small, intensely rendered part stand for the whole is characteristic of his vision. Rousseau's power of abbreviation constantly advances as he strives for larger expression.

The sentiment of flowers was strong in him. Later in 1908 when he was painting the portrait of Guillaume Apollinaire and Marie Laurencin (*The Muse Inspiring the Poet*) he instructed his friend to purchase sweet william (*l'œillet de poète*) and when gilliflowers (*giroflées*) turned up instead and got themselves painted into the picture, he insisted on doing a second version with the correct flowers in place.

By 1895 Rousseau was known to many leading artists. Through constant exhibition in the Independents (where every year he trundled his canvases to the Salon in a little cart) he had slowly won the interest of a new generation beginning to be concerned with invented rather than observed forms. As early as 1890 Maurice Denis had written: "Remember that a picture—before it is a war horse, a nude woman or an anecdote—is essentially a plane surface covered with colors arranged in a certain order." Among others Paul Sérusier and Charles Guérin made his acquaintance and in 1893 he was introduced to Degas at the Gauguin exhibition. According to Vollard, Degas, on another occasion, bored by the many new theories expounded at the Independents, suddenly turned round and pointed at a picture. "Why shouldn't that be the painter of the future?" It was a work by Rousseau. When a prominent art critic was preparing a volume on the leading artists of the day, Rousseau appeared at the publisher's with the following biographical sketch[1] along with a self-portrait drawn in ink (page 23).

"Born at Laval in the year 1844, in view of the lack of wealth of his parents was obliged to follow at first another career than that to which his artistic taste called him.

[1] First published by Soupault (bibl. 139) and in Wilenski (bibl. 165) from which the present translation comes. A facsimile of the original appears on the back fly leaf.

Self-Portrait. 1895. Pen and ink.
Collection Antonio Santamarina, Buenos Aires.

"So it was only in 1885 that he made his beginnings in art after many mortifications, alone, with only nature as a teacher, and some advice received from Gérôme and Clément. His first two creations were sent to the Salon at the Champs Elysées. They were entitled 'An Italian Dance' and 'Sunset.' In the following year he created further 'Carnival Evening' and 'A Thunderstroke.' Thereafter followed 'Waiting,' 'A Poor Devil,' 'After the Feast,' 'Parting,' 'Dinner on the Lawn,' 'The Suicide,' 'To My Father,' 'Myself, Portrait-landscape of the Author,' 'Tiger Pursuing Explorers,' 'Centenary of Independence,' 'Liberty,' 'The Last of the Fifty-first,' 'War,' a genre portrait of the writer A. J., also about two hundred drawings in pen and pencil, and a certain number of landscapes of Paris and environs. It was only after hard experiences that he managed to make himself known from among the many artists surrounding him. He has perfected himself more and more in the original manner which he has adopted and is becoming one of our best realist painters. As a characteristic mark he wears bushy whiskers and has joined with the Independents long since, believing that all liberty to create must be left to the inventor whose thoughts are elevated to the beautiful and the good. He will never forget the members of the press who have known how to understand him in times of discouragement and who have helped him to become the man he should be.

Written in Paris, 10th of July, '95
HENRI ROUSSEAU"

War. 1894. Oil, 44½ x 76⅛ inches. Collection E. Bignou, Paris.

Such simplicity tempted tricks. Friends convinced him that the President of the Republic had invited him to dinner. On another occasion a man dressed as Puvis de Chavannes (then a great figure in the Paris art world) visited the humble studio. "I have been waiting for you a long time," remarked Rousseau as he graciously showed the imposter his recent canvases.

In the 'nineties Rousseau also met Alfred Jarry, the Bohemian author of *Ubu-Roi*. They were both natives of Laval, where Rousseau had known Jarry's father. The meeting is said to have taken place at the Independents, where Rousseau was standing beside his pictures. Instantly impressed by their strangeness, Jarry commissioned a portrait. Complete with parrot and chameleon the picture made its appearance in the Independents of 1894. (As early as 1891 Rousseau had exhibited a portrait of Pierre Loti with a cat, but since there is no record that he knew Loti, the picture may have been done from a photograph or newspaper cut.)

Through Jarry, Rousseau was introduced to Rémy de Gourmont who ordered a lithograph for the magazine, *L'Imagier*. This — his only print [1] — is connected with a canvas of *War* shown in 1894. For the catalog Rousseau wrote the following legend: "Frightful, she passes, leaving in her wake, despair, tears and ruin." Though once a soldier, Rousseau hated war. "If a King wants to wage war let a mother go to him and forbid it," he often remarked.

This lithograph, with its strongly Expressionist tendencies, continues the sense of movement first attempted in *Storm in the Jungle* (page 17).

At times this desire for movement within the canvas is abandoned for an intensified striving toward the monumental. The severely frontal *Portrait of a Young Girl* (page 26) shows him seeking to bind figure and landscape into firmer union. The straight up and down pose is repeated again and again in the tree trunks, giving the composition a primitive verticality. Undoubtedly the model belonged to the *petit bourgeois* circles of the Plaisance quarter but as was his custom in portraits he devised a special out-of-door setting. There is something touching in Rousseau's struggle to surround this maiden with the symbols of pastoralism. The sheep at her feet, the trees in young leaf, the distant, lighted sky are painted with the same exactitude as the yellow boots and impassive face. At about this period the artist exhibited several portraits of children in the Independents. *Boy on Rocks* (page 27) may be one of them. Rousseau had a particular fondness for children, whom he portrayed in all their dignity and intensity. Undoubtedly he was influenced by the cabinet photograph, but nothing is less photographic than the result. The artist's increasing interest in a few clear forms turns the velvet suit, striped dress, and stockings into a striking pattern. The "Alpine" landscape repeating the lines of the figure may derive from the fortifications around Paris. In another portrait such "rocks" were so explained by Rousseau.

[1] See front fly leaf of this catalog where it is reproduced in the example belonging to Jean Goriany.

Portrait of a Young Girl. 1893–95. Oil, 24 x 18 inches. Collection Philadelphia Museum of Art.

In a series of landscapes Rousseau now attempts to paint with a broader touch. One of his heritages from the folk tradition was the linear marking-off of a canvas. Strong lines divide the surface into areas to be filled with color, almost in the manner of a mosaic. But the more he probed nature and came in contact with other paintings, the more Rousseau realized that too much of the linear, like too much ornamentation, may reduce the force of a picture. Unconsciously, perhaps, he was working towards that sustained unity found in the background of *The Sleeping Gypsy* of 1897 (page 33).

In some of his views of the Parc Montsouris done about this time, he strives for a more painter-like approach. Instead of defining each leaf he indicates a tree as a mass, then

Boy on Rocks. 1895–97. Oil, 21½ x 17¾ inches. The Chester Dale Collection (Lent to the Philadelphia Museum of Art).

builds up its modeling with a broad stroke or stipple. Edges tend to lose their crispness, and a generalized shape replaces the once complicated detail.

Unconsciously but definitely Rousseau begins to obtain more feeling of depth. Painting in superimposed flat planes remained always his favorite way of composing but at this period he explores varous devices of perspective. The tilting plane of the river in *Footbridge at Passy* (page 28) adds a dimension that many of his early landscapes lacked. He avoids exact balance, learning better how to echo a dark mass with a light or to return movement with counter-movement. Broader zones of color are made to answer their complements.

Artillerymen (page 29) belongs with the canvases of *War* (exhibited 1894) and *The*

27

Footbridge at Passy (La Passerelle de Passy). 1895. Oil, 17½ x 20 inches. Collection Morton R. Goldsmith.

Last of the 51st (exhibited 1893 and now lost) to that brief period when Rousseau turned towards military themes. One suspects a group photograph as the basis for the picture. But the set arrangement of the soldiers and the stressed darks and lights are employed by Rousseau with a wholly fresh insight. The landscape, as usual, is carefully keyed to the pattern of figures.

All the knowledge that Rousseau had added to his natural gift, all the freedoms he had gained by ten years of intense labor are incorporated into his greatest painting of the 'nineties, *The Sleeping Gypsy* (page 33), exhibited at the Independents in 1897. For such works "he had perfected himself more and more in the original manner which he adopted" and such a picture was intended to prove him "one of our best realist painters."

Realism is not the first quality one attributes to *The Sleeping Gypsy*. But its painter consciously meant it to be a naturalistic work. Here, I believe, he tried to rival his mentor,

28

Artillerymen. c. 1895. Oil, 32 x 39½ inches. Collection The Solomon R. Guggenheim Foundation.

Gérôme, famous for African subjects with wild animals portrayed in bare stretches of landscape. Gérôme's canvas, *The Caravan*, shows a tiger watching the advance of a desert party from his lonely promontory, and *The Two Majesties* depicts a lion (curiously like the beast in Rousseau's canvas) gazing at the setting sun which casts its clear orange beams across a sandy waste.

We know Rousseau's respect for meticulous painting of this sort. He greatly admired Bouguereau and Courtois, pointing out to amused friends their perfection of finish. But labor as he might to equal their effects, *The Sleeping Gypsy* is not another Salon machine. Unconsciously Rousseau created the subject in his own manner, making use of Gérôme's material as he made use of nature, not to copy its detail but to recast and reconstruct its elements.

In place of Gérôme's skilled description Rousseau gives us a vision expressed in purely

Tiger Hunt. 1895–97. Oil, 15 x 18⅛ inches. Collection The Columbus Gallery of Fine Arts. Ferdinand Howald Collection.

plastic terms. As in *Carnival Evening* (frontispiece), painted eleven years before, it is the artist's organizing imagination at work which lends the picture its power. But where the earlier painting stressed the lyricism of night and masquerade, this canvas instantly sets up an uncanny, dream-like mood. The delicate forms of Rousseau's style of the 'eighties are replaced by forms of such grandeur that inevitably one compares them to some French classic master of the past. Here the enrichment of surface is limited to a few areas like the striped robe of the gypsy and the lion's mane. The fixed, dramatic tension between animal and figure is heightened by the play of large planes set in vast space; the harmony of color, reinforced by the moonlight, binding the forms together in a highly abstract way. Finally, it is the indissoluble union of design and poetry that makes *The Sleeping Gypsy* one of the strangest and most moving paintings in all of modern art.

Rousseau himself thought so well of the picture that he offered the canvas to his birth-

30

place for a moderate sum.[1] Presumably it was sent to Laval but never hung. (It would be interesting to imagine its reception in this provincial French town at the end of the last century.) But though Laval rejected it, the painting was to become a forerunner of several twentieth-century developments. The motif of mandolin and vase (see detail, page 32) suggests later still lifes by Picasso and Braque. Its trance-like character foretells Surrealism and was especially influential when in 1926, after long years of disappearance, the picture was shown in an exhibition of the John Quinn collection in Paris. Jean Cocteau celebrated its rediscovery in a typical prose-poem in which he suggests that the lion and the landscape are a projection of the gypsy's dream and not thought of as actually present—an interpretation which seems more characteristic of the Surrealism of the moment than the method of Rousseau in 1897. Wilenski notes that De Chirico's *Lion and Gladiators* (1927, Detroit Institute of Arts) stems from it.

The *Tiger Hunt* (page 30), perhaps earlier than 1897, reflects the same interest in the North African themes of Fromentin and Gérôme. Such works were painted in Rousseau's small studio where he occupied a room over a plasterer's shop. His second wife had died and there he lived alone, composing his poems and dramas (page 74) and founding a "Philotechnical Association" to teach all the arts. Since his youth he had played the flute, mandolin and cornet and performed so adequately on the violin that he was hired for con-

[1] The original letter from Rousseau to the Mayor of Laval has come to light. It was published in *Le Petit Journal*, Paris, January 7, 1935. A photostat of it in the painter's own handwriting has been kindly forwarded to me by James Johnson Sweeney from Henri Pierre Roché who bought the painting for John Quinn. It reads:

July 10, 1898

To Monsieur le Maire,

I have the honor of sending you these few lines as a compatriot of yours who has become a self-taught artist and is desirous that his native city possess one of his works, proposing that you purchase from me a genre painting called *The Sleeping Gypsy* (*La Bohémienne endormie*) which measures 2.60 in width by 1.90 meters in height [Ed. dimensions of frame]. A wandering negress, playing the mandolin, with her jar beside her (vase containing drinking water), sleeps deeply, worn out by fatigue. A lion wanders by, detects her and doesn't devour her. There's an effect of moonlight, very poetic. The scene takes place in a completely arid desert. The Gypsy is dressed in Oriental fashion.

I will let it go for 2,000 to 1,800 francs because I would be happy that the city of Laval possess a remembrance of one of its children.

In the hope that my offer will be treated with favor, accept, Monsieur le Maire, the assurance of my distinguished consideration.

HENRI ROUSSEAU
Artist Painter
3 Rue Vercingétorix
Paris.

Across the top is written (in another hand): Brought to the attention of the Director of the Museum. Laval, July 15, 1898. The Mayor.

Inclosed was a calling card: Henri Rousseau
Artist Painter
Wednesdays, 2 to 5 o'clock. 3 rue Vercingétorix

(The name and the words "Artist Painter" are printed along with the address 14, Avenue du Maine, which had been crossed out. "3 rue Vercingétorix" and "Wednesdays, 2 to 5 o'clock" are in the painter's handwriting.)

Henri Rousseau
1897

Mandolin and Vase, detail from The Sleeping Gypsy. This section of the canvas points forward to certain Cubist still lifes by Picasso and Braque.

The Sleeping Gypsy. 1897 (dated). Oil, 51 x 70 inches. Collection The Museum of Modern Art, New York. Gift of Mrs. Simon Guggenheim.

Landscape, Outskirts of Paris (Paysage de Banlieue, Environs de Paris). *1898–1900.* **Oil,** *15 x 18 inches. Collection The Cleveland Museum of Art.*

certs in the Tuileries Gardens. His prospectus advertises courses in music, diction, painting and drawing for children and adults. On Thursday evenings he conducted a sketch class from the model. The fee was eight francs a month, later raised to ten. He occasionally received commissions for portraits, even trading pictures to his baker or grocer.

1898–1906

The Sleeping Gypsy marks a turning point in Rousseau's career. In it he finally joined the geometry of the folk style to his own freer conventions of drawing and color. The expressional content of folk painting has been enlarged into an individual expression. Starting with a limited repertory of visual symbols, the artist, with infinite patience and intuitive understanding, has finally developed his personal language. From now on there is **no**

35

Street Scene (sketch for View of Malakoff). *1898. Oil, 7½ x 11¼ inches. Collection Max Weber.*

longer that sign of struggle with architectonics or poetry, often found in preceding works. Rousseau moves easily in the world of his creation, *realizing* (in the sense that Cézanne used the word) as easily and clearly as he imagines.

With a few notable exceptions this period is one of resting. After the intense effort of carrying through a few large paintings, Rousseau turns to smaller things. To the Independents he sends chiefly little landscapes and portraits. The landscapes are apt to include in their titles the time of year (*View of the Bois de Boulogne* [*autumn*]) or refer to some effect of light (*Lake Dumesnil* [*setting sun*]). The best of them, like the *Landscape, Outskirts of Paris* (page 35), contain clear blue skies, fluttering clouds, green trees, rose and red and gray houses, but though Rousseau remains faithful to local colors, there is an atmospheric envelopment very different from the earlier concentration on a few flat tones and severe boundaries. If, in their muted harmonies and fineness of feeling, such landscapes at times recall Corot just back from his first Italian trip, on other occasions their perfection of hue and cool light remind us of the early Sisley and Pissarro. But beneath softer contours and freer brushwork still lies Rousseau's sense of completeness.

View of Malakoff. 1898 (dated). Oil, 18 x 21¾ inches. Collection A. Villard, Paris.

From about this time come his first painted sketches from nature. Like his drawings these preliminary studies before the motif have not been popular with critics seeking to celebrate Rousseau as an inspired "primitive." As a matter of fact, from the first Rousseau had been curiously dependent upon the object. Now he began to make on the spot, quick, summary sketches which he would later take back to the studio and rework into finished landscapes.

These sketches show a new side of Rousseau's abilities, since they are painted in a deft, Impressionist technique, with hazy, soft edges, dusky shadows and trembling lights. He did not think of them as pictures but as indications for pictures. He never approved of highly finished sketches or sketchy paintings. They show that had he wished, he might have excelled as an Impressionist. There is a charm in their green or gray tone, and a special sensitivity in their casual effects of light. The handling is easy and spontaneous, showing how remarkable was the artist's first response to nature.

In his studio Rousseau would compose his landscape somewhat on the basis of the sketch. Where everything appeared blurred or softly brushed together, he would clarify and separate. This method has been compared to Seurat's but the likeness is superficial. Seurat's little sketches before nature were fragments of experience, analyzed according to a highly scientific theory of color contrasts and comparisons. Rousseau's were rapid, total impressions, made to fix the main shapes and color areas of the motif. Where Seurat eventually wove dozens of such little *croquetons* into one magisterial composition, Rousseau let these brief records stand for nature in the studio. How drastically he made them over may be seen by comparing a sketch (page 36) with the completed landscape (page 37).

In 1899 and 1900 Rousseau did not exhibit in the Salon of the Independents, but in 1901 he showed what is presumably the composition of a nude maiden, bear and hunter, entitled *An Unpleasant Surprise* (Mauvaise surprise) (Barnes Foundation, Merion, Pa.).[1] It carries on the monumental dream qualities of *The Sleeping Gypsy* and elicited, according to Vollard, considerable admiration from Renoir. "What a beautiful tone in that picture by Rousseau," the painter remarked, "and the female nude . . . I'm sure that even Ingres wouldn't have disliked that!" The mention of Ingres in connection with growing appreciation of Rousseau comes at a time when the early nineteenth-century classical masters, long despised, were being rehabilitated. In 1902 Maurice Denis published his famous essay on the pupils of Ingres, calling attention to Ingres' early enthusiasm for Italian primitives at Assisi and Perugia, and stressing his artistic doctrine, which recognized the role of naiveté. In opposition to such reborn classicism there was everywhere a growing interest in exoticism and the exotic arts, one manifestation of which can be found in the emergence of the *Fauves*. Rousseau in 1904 sent to the Independents his *Scouts Attacked by a Tiger* (Barnes Foundation, Merion, Pa.), probably the first of his tropical compositions since *Storm in the Jungle* of 1891. (The same tiger appears in both.) And at about this period he painted the two small jungle scenes (pages 40 and 41), so close in size and complementary in mood that he perhaps intended them as a pair.

The contrast with Rousseau's early use of such material is significant. In place of detailed forms sharp with drawing, we find sensitively painted silhouettes crisscrossing and overlapping against the light. Gone are the frenzy of mood and the movement of planes. All is quiet, mysterious and poised. The hours of twilight and moonlight, with great beasts half hidden in the jungle, provide an opportunity for him to express that fantasy which, especially since *The Sleeping Gypsy*, had been a commanding element in everything he did.

The enormous and mural-like painting, *The Hungry Lion . . .*, shown at the new Autumn Salon of 1905, suddenly focused attention upon the painter. This was the famous Salon of the *Fauves*. A gallery was set aside for their work and one critic, Louis Vauxcelles, chris-

[1] Usually dated 1891.

38

*Owl. c. 1905. Oil on wood, 9¾ x 6
inches. Collection Paul Petit, Paris.*

Bird of Prey, detail of The Hungry Lion . . .
Collection Dr. Franz Meyer, Zürich.

(Comparison from Egger, bibl. 19)

tened it "a cage of wild beasts," a better description of Rousseau's own entry a few rooms
away. By being shown not in an enormous and indiscriminate exhibit but in the company
of Manet, Toulouse-Lautrec and Redon, and along with the revolutionary young *Fauves*,
Rousseau finally seemed to relate to the experimental movements of the nineteenth and
twentieth centuries rather than to an eccentric and old-fashioned idiom. Myopic critics
might still pronounce his work "ridiculous," but young painters like Delaunay, Vlaminck,
Marie Laurencin and Picasso, and writers like Guillaume Apollinaire and André Salmon
began to be fascinated with the man as well as his art.

In Rousseau's personality this generation pretended to discover all the virtues of the
"primitive soul" which Gauguin had traveled so far to find, and best of all these virtues
could be experienced here in Paris, no farther away than the rue Perrel. They remembered
that in forming his own style Gauguin had consulted the *images d'Epinal*, and they began
to seek out the work of the self-taught and to extol it.

This sudden interest in Rousseau was part of a wider return to historic sources, which
characterizes so much of the advanced artistic experiment of our century. His impeccable
technique led them back to French and Italian primitives while his intuitive inventions
helped to justify their own conscious experiment. At first they treated him with a half-
loving condescension. Max Weber recalls Rousseau's appearance at the elder Madame
Delaunay's salon, a small, modest figure, with a sweet piping voice and the simplicity of a

Jungle with a Lion. 1904–06. Oil, 14¾ x 18 inches. Collection The Museum of Modern Art, New York. The Lillie P. Bliss Collection.

The Jungle: Lion and Buffalo. 1904–06. Oil, 14¾ x 17½ inches. Collection Mr. and Mrs. Sam A. Lewisohn.

Banks of the Oise. 1905. Oil, 18 x 22 inches. Collection The Smith College Museum of Art.

The Goatherd. 1905–07 (?). Oil, 16¼ x 21¼ inches. Collection James Thrall Soby.

House, Outskirts of Paris. 1905–07. Oil, 13¾ x 18¼ inches. Collection Max Weber.

child. This was the man who represented in the flesh what the young sophisticates had named *le style concierge*.

Aside from establishing his reputation and marking the theme which was to engross Rousseau for the last five years of his life, *The Hungry Lion . . .* has a deeper interest, for it furnishes another clue to his method. A sketch of an owl (evidently made from life) has survived (page 39) which Rousseau later made over into a bird of prey and set among the leaves of his great composition (detail, page 39). It is instructive to follow the subtle changes in design and feeling by which this transformation took place.

In later landscapes the note of fantasy, ever stronger, expresses itself in a freer association of forms and in richer implications of color and texture. In addition *Banks of the Oise* (page 42) and *House, Outskirts of Paris* (above) possess the dream-like serenity of some of the jungle compositions. (A preliminary sketch from nature for the latter picture belongs to Professor E. R. Weiss of Berlin.) The vibrant stippling of the trees in *Landscape, Pontoise* (page 45) reminds one of the dotted touch of the Pointillists, without their broken color. Perhaps Rousseau responded, unconsciously, to some such influence, but he

44

Landscape, Pontoise. 1906 (dated). Oil, 15½ x 12½ inches. Collection Mrs. William Hale Harkness.

Henri Rousseau. From a photograph owned by Max Weber. Inscribed: "Gift to my friend Weber artist-painter. Paris 14/12, 1908. Henri Rousseau artist-painter."

put it to far different use. He was still strongly moved to objectify, having such unyielding respect for every object in nature that he wished to convey the sense of each leaf, if only by the briefest indication. Such late landscapes, lit with romantic light and exquisite in color, contrast markedly with the spare and geometricized city views of the 'nineties. *Banks of the Oise,* moreover, contains a curious telescoping of several motifs, combined into an imaginative unity which leads directly on to the artist's last phase.

1907–1910

Now commenced the fullest period of Rousseau's life. His dream had come true. At the age of sixty-three he found himself in the center of the most advanced group of artists and writers in Paris, admired and recognized by the intellectual world. In 1907 he received his first large commission from Madame Delaunay for the *Snake-Charmer,* now in the Louvre. Its exhibition in the Autumn Salon brought him wide fame. But nothing turned his head. He still remained the ingenuous "artist-painter," accepting applause with the same tranquillity with which he had met abuse. Though he had acquired a dealer, Joseph Brummer, who was able to sell a few works for him now and then for small sums, he remained poor all his life, hardly knowing (as his letters prove) where his next meal was coming from.

"Having my rent to pay, then a big bill at my color merchant's, I am very short of money and this evening I have only 15 centimes for supper." (Letter to Apollinaire, April 28, 1909.)

Max Weber, who as an art student in Paris at the time knew him intimately, has described his studio. Rousseau lived in a single room with a large window. There he painted, slept and did his modest cooking. On the wall was a plaster cast of an Egyptian relief (for him all supreme art was "Egyptian," including the paintings of Gauguin and Picasso) and over his cot hung *Present and Past*, a curious double portrait of himself and his second wife. A hideous statue on a pedestal, his violin, a few chairs and a red sofa, soon to be immortalized in the canvas, *The Dream* (page 68), made up the other furnishings. All about him were pictures, and when a visitor asked if it was not uncomfortable to sleep in a studio he replied, "You know, when I wake up I can smile at my canvases."

There he painted in a trance-like stillness from morning to night, slowly proceeding from the top to the bottom of his canvas. A picture might take two or three months and he was in luck if he received a hundred francs for it. Sometimes, Apollinaire relates, when he was engaged in a fantastic subject, he was overcome with fear and rushed trembling to open a window. On another occasion he told his biographer, Wilhelm Uhde, that his hand was being guided by the spirit of his departed wife. When Uhde met Rousseau for the first time, the *Snake-Charmer* was on his easel. "I realized already that the legend of his artistic 'naïveté' was unjustified. He was concerned with the general harmony and balance of the

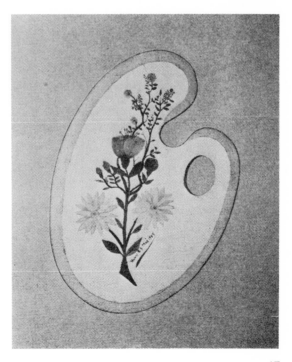

Rousseau's Palette. 1907 (dated). Wood, 8⅞ x 6⅞ inches. Collection Mrs. John D. Rockefeller, Jr.

Merry Jesters (Joyeux Farceurs). *1906. Oil, 57 x 44 inches. Collection Mr. and Mrs. Walter Conrad Arensberg.*

48

The Jungle: Tiger Attacking a Buffalo. 1908 (dated). Oil, 67½ x 75 inches. Lent by Mrs. Patrick C. Hill to the Joseph Winterbotham Collection of The Art Institute of Chicago.

large composition and asked my advice whether to make a tone darker or lighter, whether to suppress something here or add something there."

Occasionally Rousseau visited the Louvre and discussed the paintings afterwards with nice understanding. "Which ones did you like best?" he was asked. "You see there are so many of them I forget the names," Rousseau replied. Brummer recalls that he mentioned only Courbet with admiration. (*Boat by a Cliff*, formerly in the collection of Paul Guillaume, Paris, seems to recall Courbet.) He conscientiously attended the official Salon where he led his pupils before the most academic examples. To the end of his life Bouguereau remained his idol and Bouguereau's death is said to have affected him deeply. At the Cézanne Memorial of 1907 his comment was, "You know, I could finish all these pictures."

The artist loved festivity and during the years 1908 and 1909 organized a series of musical soirées in his studio. Special invitations were sent out and a hand-decorated program given to each guest. Several descriptions of these events have appeared in print, of which the most precise is Adolph Basler's (translated from bibl. 20):

It was with Max Weber that I sometimes went to the soirées in the rue Perrel. This American, a tenor who apparently had sung in synagogues, was the chief soloist of these friendly affairs where artists elbowed the people of the neighborhood. I noticed, among the guests, the baker with his daughter who was taking mandolin lessons from the Douanier, the little grocer round the corner, flanked by his son to whom Rousseau taught violin and drawing; the daughters of the milkman, some small business-men, a few retired inspectors from the customs and even the old eccentrics who passed their days painting by the side of their good-natured Patron. An old architect's clerk, the most persistent habitué of the place, boasted of representing the intellectual element. He teased the poor Douanier and his humble public continually. But he was the one who started the stupidest songs of the evening, particularly one threadbare old piece of the Second Empire in which all the company joined in the chorus: "Ah, Ah, Joséphine . . ."

This concert, not in the least symphonic, always began with the Marseillaise. Henri Rousseau, first violin, directed the orchestra, made up of his pupils, a mandolin, a flute, a cornet, etc. Then the grocer's son would give a recitation and the milkman's little wife would repeat the latest music hall novelty. Max Weber would sing Handel. Violin solos by the master would interlard the program with the Polka des Bébés, Cécilette *and the* Rêve d'un Ange (*mazurka*).

These gatherings ("informal and artistic" Rousseau called them) were attended by the intelligentsia as well as artists. Georges Duhamel, Jules Romains, Francis Carco and always Guillaume Apollinaire could be found with Picasso, Braque, Max Jacob and the critics, André Warnod and Maurice Raynal. Foreigners (all foreigners were "Americans" to Rousseau) like the Russians, Baroness Oettingen (who painted under the name of Angiboult and as "Roch Grey" later wrote a poetic volume on the artist), her brother Serge Jastrebzoff (Ferat), the German critic and art dealer, Uhde, the Italian painter, Ardengo Soffici, were constant guests. When Max Weber was about to leave for America, a special soirée was given on December 19, 1908. During this period Rousseau's "Saturdays" became almost as celebrated as Mallarmé's "Tuesdays" in the rue de Rome had once been.

So great was the interest in Rousseau on the part of the younger artists that in 1908 a fantastic "banquet" was tendered in his honor in Picasso's studio in the rue Ravignan. Picasso had picked up an early portrait (*Mlle M.*) by Rousseau for a few francs in a junk shop and this became the excuse for a more or less spontaneous party where, in addition to many of Rousseau's friends already mentioned, the company included Leo and Gertrude Stein. The evening was a gay one, even though dinner failed to appear, Picasso having given the wrong date to the caterer. There were extravagant toasts and speeches, Rousseau

A Game of Football (Joueurs de Football). *1908 (dated). Oil, 40 x 32 inches. Collection Mrs. Murray S. Danforth.*

played on his violin, the guests sang, and Apollinaire improvised a poem beginning, "You remember, Rousseau, the Aztec landscape. . . ." The painter was overcome with emotion, and the tears ran down his face as he listened to the praise of his admirers.

Though Rousseau now concentrated on exotic landscapes, finding a ready response for them which in turn encouraged him to paint more and more ambitiously, he varied his excursions into these fantasies with occasional pieces of genre. Only Rousseau, with his folk sincerity and self-taught principles of composition, could have carried through to success *A Game of Football* (page 51) shown at the Independents in 1908. There is something festive and ballet-like in these four figures seen against a luminous autumn landscape reminiscent of other richly surfaced views of the same time. Against the squared-off field, with rows of trees placed at either side like columns, the players, in striped jerseys, are depicted in jaunty movement, their poses rhythmically linked, one to another, the staccato of the hands repeated in four distant trees. Judged by the standards of Salon realism, *A Game of Football* was a preposterous affair, and there were many to judge it such, among them certain admirers who had learned to accept the stylizations of his tropical landscapes. To those who saw deeper the picture could be related to the traditions of Tournai tapestries and the frescoes at Avignon.

The Cart of Père Juniet (page 53), painted the same year, is one of Rousseau's most clarified and subtle translations of that middle-class milieu which made up his daily life. By comparing it with a photograph [1] of the models one can see how the painter managed at the same time to enlarge the spatial significance, order the color, and still preserve to an extraordinary degree the poetic homeliness of the original subject. Max Weber, who watched him paint it, relates that at one time when he saw the picture on the easel, all of the canvas was covered with the exception of a white space left for the dog underneath the cart. "Aren't you making that dog too large?" he inquired. Rousseau looked musingly at the picture. "No, it must be that way," was the painter's answer. It is this intuitive certainty of the rightness or wrongness of a pictorial element which more and more marks the final development of Rousseau's art.

His happiness was rudely shattered early in 1909 when he became mixed up with an unscrupulous former pupil who used the aged painter in a scheme to cheat the Bank of France.[2] The swindle was discovered; and though obviously innocent, Rousseau found himself haled into court and facing a serious charge. Terrified, the painter is said to have offered his counsel the whole contents of his studio, with its many unsold canvases, if he would only get him off. At the trial the lawyer produced the artist's scrapbook with its long series of damaging *critiques* and, to the surprise and hilarity of the court, displayed one of his pictures, *Monkeys in the Forest*, to show what a hopeless innocent the defendant was. But the Bank of France is a serious institution and Rousseau was found guilty and sen-

---

[1] A comparison made by J. J. Sweeney in his *Plastic Redirections in Twentieth Century Painting*, Chicago, The University of Chicago Press, 1934, p. 15 and reproduced here by his kind permission.

[2] Wilenski (bibl. 165) gives the only full account of this episode, page 245, and Appendix IV, 376–7.

The Cart of Père Juniet. 1908 (dated). Oil, 38¼ x 50¾ inches. Collection Madame Paul Guillaume, Paris.

Photograph of the Juniet family and the cart. Courtesy of James Johnson Sweeney.

*Mother and Child. 1905–08 (?) Oil, 8¾ x 6½ inches. Collection
Max Weber.*

tenced to two years' imprisonment. Fortunately the sentence was remanded. Bowing to the
judge, the relieved artist remarked, "I thank you deeply, Monsieur le Président, I will
paint the portrait of your wife."

An increased freedom to move within the picture space and still retain a simple, domi-
nant design is found again in the small canvas, *Mother and Child* (above). Two flowering
branches, in place of elaborated trees, bend over the heads of the figures, and notes of sal-

54

Still Life. 1900–08 (?). Oil on wood, 2⅞ x 5½ inches. Collection Max Weber.

mon, vermilion and blue are instinctively balanced by the gleaming black of the mother's dress. The little still life (above) with its sensitive color and impeccable clarity show his respect for the object, no matter how humble. The mouse gnawing at the candle is a characteristic touch. On its reverse is an inscription: "Gift to my friend Weber, the 20th of August, 1908, union of America and France, the 2 republics."

The *Portrait of Joseph Brummer* of 1909 (page 59), one of the last he did, shows his friend and dealer seated in a wicker chair before a background of trees, closely allied to the extravagant foliage of the jungles. It is a mistake to think of such a setting as merely a decorative convention to fill space. For Rousseau the landscape element was quite as important as the figure. When engaged on the portrait of Apollinaire, the artist selected a background from the Luxembourg Gardens. "I've found a pretty corner, very poetic." (Letter of August 31, 1908.) The poet appeared for his first sitting and the artist carefully measured "my nose, my mouth, my ears, my forehead, my hands, reducing them to the dimensions of the stretcher." This method of working, which suggests a tailor rather than a painter, has been often quoted to prove Rousseau's incredible naïveté. But such an obeisance to reality liberated him for his significant problem: how to objectify the figure before him and still harmonize it with those strict pictorial laws which his intuition demanded. Except in the little sketches before nature, his method was never instantaneous. It was a slow, additive exploration. Organizing his impressions into broad planes, he continually strove for greater clarity. To Uhde he remarked of a picture in process, "Don't you believe I ought to make the leaves in the first plane a little clearer?" His feeling for the permanent

Fisherman. 1909–10. Oil, 14½ x 17½ inches. Collection Dr. and Mrs. Harry Bakwin.

made him seek out a severe linear pattern to which he constantly opposed passages of invented color and relieving areas of gray and black. The picture was not finished until every form had its proper stability and tension.

In a way he was as lost as Cézanne without nature. During the course of the portrait his letters to Apollinaire implore him to come to the studio to pose. The background is done but the figure needs more attention; the paint will dry in and then it will be double the work. "I have had many difficulties . . . You didn't come back to pose and I was bothered about certain tones but I finished it, nevertheless, from memory." (Letter of August 3, 1909, page 75.) He demanded the model before him to check and control his vision. Lacking it, he could not realize the individuality of forms, the special sense of their character. "Never forget nature, Weber," he used to remark again and again to the young painter.

By the time he portrayed Joseph Brummer he knew just how to proceed. Compare the reworked face of the *Portrait of a Young Girl* (page 26) with the broadly designed features in this later example. The feeling for grandeur which permeates his final style condenses

56

Spring in the Valley of the Bièvre. 1908–10 (?). Oil, 21½ x 18 inches. Collection The Metropolitan Museum of Art.

the multiplicity of nature into a solid, monumental expression. Psychologically the model is invested with the calm but intense gentleness that we find in all of Rousseau's portraits.

About this time the first serious, if somewhat ironic, consideration of Rousseau to appear in print was published in *Comœdia* for April 3, 1909 (bibl. 10). The writer was an official critic, Arsène Alexandre, but he went so far as to admit that "if they weren't so expensive I would like to have some of these pictures, not to hang them up on the wall, for they exercise a dangerous fascination, but to look at from time to time when we need to be reminded of sincerity. If he had possessed the thing he was utterly lacking in: knowledge, and if he had been able, at the same time to preserve his freshness of conception, Rousseau would be the Paolo Uccello of our century."

The final year of Rousseau's life was an extremely full one. Uhde and Vollard had begun to buy his pictures. Three of his works, including the *Merry Jesters* (page 48), were shown in St. Petersburg and Rome. Though concentrating on jungle themes, he continued his portraits and city views up to the very end, still setting down his first impressions for landscape in preliminary sketches.

Comparison of sketch and finished picture (pages 60 and 61) gives us valuable insight into his way of working. The little study before nature is a rapidly brushed reaction to the scene. The main masses of dark and light are already established but not in any positive arrangement. This quick and ragged brushwork makes no concession to the demands of picture-making. There it differs strikingly from the apparently negligent, but often exquisite touch of the Impressionists. However, this capturing of atmosphere, this blurring and running together of form, ally it to the methods of Impressionism. The slaty blues and grays and fastidious touches of black might almost have been dashed down by Manet.

Rousseau now starts to build. The sketchy contours are stiffened, made more regular. All that he feels about one of his favorite spots in Paris makes him wish to create a permanent statement. New verticals are introduced, relating the motif to the frame, and the whole composition is given a fulcrum by moving the little figure directly to the center. Only a few lines are used but these lock the linear pattern securely. (Note, for example, how a tree in the middle has been given a triangular shape to repeat in reverse the ship's rigging, and how the arc of the bridge is reiterated.) Gone is the blurred form and atmosphere. The strong illumination of the sky sharpens each silhouette and clarifies each shape. Where the color had been tonal with a tendency toward blues and greens, warm tans and browns now appear to complete the harmony. The red note of the flag (the addition of which plays so vital a part in the design) does much to balance the greens, adding as well its note of animation.

Subtly Rousseau flattens out the uncertain space of the sketch into a system of parallel planes and sensitive intervals. The windows, the highlights on the trees and the rings on the parapet are related in a new rhythm. Seeing the sketch and completed picture side by side reveals again how the artist chose his method and his own stylizations.

58

Portrait of Joseph Brummer. 1909 (dated). Oil, 45¾ x 35 inches. Collection Dr. Franz Meyer, Zürich. On extended loan to The Museum of Modern Art, New York.

Notre Dame from the Quai Henri-Quatre. 1909. Oil, 8½ x 11 inches. Collection Mrs. Henry D. Sharpe.

Such stylizations reach their climax in the paintings of tropical fantasy, most of them done during the last five or six years of his life. These were the works that brought recognition in his time and established his later fame. The subjects are curiously savage. For *The Hungry Lion* . . . Rousseau wrote a poetic explanation printed in the catalog of the Autumn Salon of 1905: "The hungry lion, throwing himself upon the antelope, devours him; the panther stands by, anxiously waiting the moment when he can claim his share. Birds of prey have ripped out pieces of flesh from the poor animal who pours forth his death-cry! Setting sun." In other pictures a tiger rushes at natives or an ape attacks an Indian (page 67). It would seem that a lingering strain of Delacroix' fierce animal combats—a strain repeated in Salon painting of African and Oriental subjects down the century—makes its reappearance in Rousseau. But if the theme is the law of the jungle, the artist's development is detached and remote. The incident of the struggle is overwhelmed by a luxuriant flora which completely dominates the picture. In some of these works Rousseau treats mon-

60

Notre Dame. 1909 (dated). Oil, 13 x 16 inches. Collection The Phillips Memorial Gallery.

keys at play (pages 48 and 72) but the effect is strange and sub-humorous. His conception answers the reality of imagination rather than of nature.

In stressing Rousseau's method of composition it would be unwise to overlook his early impressions of Mexico. While he seldom mentioned his years in America, he did remark that the French soldiers were forbidden to eat the tempting fruits. Does the profusion of oranges and bananas in many pictures recall some such injunction? Rousseau referred to his jungles as "Mexican pictures" and Max Weber relates that when the Mexican Ambassador was in Paris, the painter vainly tried to reach him in an effort to sell one of his works. Furthermore one can imagine that behind the curious enlargement of leaves and flowers lie half-forgotten memories of the extraordinary landscape round Vera Cruz.

But if the impulse came to him across the years, it came not as total recall but as a feeling to be verified by nature. Scientists have identified a number of the plants in these canvases, all of them probably available at the Paris conservatory, suggesting that Rousseau

61

Vase of Flowers. 1908–09 (?). Oil, 13 x 18½ inches. Collection William S. Paley.

Flowers in a Vase. 1909 (dated). Oil, 18⅜ x 13¼ inches. Collection The Buffalo Fine Arts Academy, Albright Art Gallery.

studied his exotic flora firsthand.[1] Weber came upon him one day when he was painting. Around his palette was entwined a small branch of leaves and the artist was studying their form and color minutely. The animals, too, are readily identifiable and we know that as in the case of the owl (page 39) he made direct studies in the Zoo.

His approach was far from literal. Inspired by his vision he arbitrarily rewove the appearance of nature to suit his purpose. The long series of imaginative paintings show Rousseau obsessed by one repeated scheme of composition. He imagines a strongly lighted distance against which he silhouettes darker forms of tree or foliage. Plane upon plane is piled up in intricate design, and usually two small figures focus the eye on the foreground. This same "dream picture" haunted him from the days of *Carnival Evening* (frontispiece) to the last jungle picture he painted.

These final canvases show the self-taught artist wholly in command of his style. The minute elaboration of a passage which he loved and which in certain early pictures breaks up the larger rhythms and forms is here replaced by an all-over spatial design. If we study the right-hand section of *The Jungle: Tiger Attacking a Buffalo* (page 49), we find it amazingly complex. One cut-out plane is laid over another and yet another, but Rousseau's control is now so sure that all is directed and unified. Soffici, who watched him paint, tells us that he filled in all the greens, then all the reds, then all the blues, etc. (bibl. 135). He had conceived the picture in such precise relationship that he could estimate how many days it would take him to finish a canvas.

At last he was able to interlock figures and landscape and unite their diverse movements. The tiger in *The Jungle* (page 49) has stripes which not only repeat the surface design of the leaves, but his diagonal movement is linked with the three-dimensional broken stalks in the foreground just as the solid weight of the buffalo is bound up with the heavy bunches of bananas that hang downward. All of this takes place in a setting of tremendous magnification. A branch becomes a towering tree and flowers are as prodigiously large as lions. This distortion of natural scale lends a peculiar emotional overtone to the whole composition.

Rousseau's technique has now become free and without apparent labor. Occasionally a retouching shows where he has altered a branch or inserted a leaf but the sureness of execution matches the sureness of conception. While still preserving the effect of precise detail,

[1] Professor Charles E. Olmsted of the Department of Botany of the University of Chicago, who kindly studied photographs of several pictures, has made the following report: "The plants are conventionalized and most of them are difficult to identify. In *The Dream* (page 68) the large peltate leaves and the enormous flowers could be one of the waterlily group. The strap-shaped leaves in the lower right-hand corner belong to the genus *Sansevieria*, native to Africa, but now used extensively as a house plant in temperate regions, and probably escaped in the American tropics. In *The Jungle: Tiger Attacking a Buffalo* (page 49) the large bunches of fruit on the left and center and the very large leaves must be bananas, and the leaf just below the bunch in the center might be *Ceratozamia*, a genus of Cycads. The highly conventionalized tepee-shaped plants in *The Waterfall* (page 65) and *Exotic Landscape* (page 67) might be either *Yucca* (New World) or *Dracena* (mostly Old World). The leaves in the upper right-hand corner of the latter picture are probably those of one of the numerous palms."

The Waterfall. 1910 (dated). Oil, 45½ x 59 inches. Collection The Art Institute of Chicago. Helen Birch Bartlett Memorial.

Exotic Landscape: Ape and Indian. 1910 (dated). Oil, 45 x 64 inches. Private collection, Chicago.

67

Detail of The Dream. *Collection Sidney Janis.*

Exotic Landscape. 1910 (dated). Oil, 51 x 64 inches. Collection Colonel Robert R. McCormick.

midst of a jungle. This mixture of incongruous elements surprised even his friends and caused a sensation in the Independents. To a critic, André Dupont, who wrote for an explanation, Rousseau replied: "The sleeping woman on the sofa dreams that she is transported into the forest, hearing the music of the snake-charmer. This explains why the sofa is in the picture." But though the motif was thus cleared up for the literal, Rousseau was so much the artist that to André Salmon he confided: "The sofa is there only because of its glowing, red color."

The Dream is a summation of all those qualities which make Rousseau inimitable. Its organization of spaces and complex tones (an artist counted over fifty variations of green alone) is equaled by its sentiment. The plane of reality (the figure on the sofa) is inventively joined to the plane of the dream (the jungle). In it appears, in heightened form, every symbol of the last ten years of Rousseau's life, redesigned and related with a free intensity. The nude figure surrounded by enormous lilies is one of Rousseau's most perfect realizations (detail, page 70), while the leopards peering from the jungle leaves are full of his expressive mystery (detail, page 71).

"Tell me, M. Rousseau," Vollard asked him, "how did you get so much air to circulate among those trees and the moonlight to look so real?"

"By observing nature, M. Vollard," replied the painter, true to his ideal to the last.

As he prepared the picture for exhibition, Rousseau expressed himself as pleased. To Apollinaire he wrote: "I have just sent off my big picture; everyone likes it. I hope that you are going to employ your literary talents to avenge me for all the insults and injuries I have received." (March 11, 1910.) These words, spoken at the end of his life, are one of the few indications we have of how much Rousseau had suffered from being misunderstood.

On September 4, 1910, he died at a hospital in Paris at the age of sixty-six. His friends were out of the city and only seven people attended his funeral, among them Paul Signac, President of the Independents. A year later a tombstone was set up by Robert Delaunay, Apollinaire and M. Quéval, his landlord. And in 1913 Brancusi and the painter Ortiz de Zarate engraved on the stone the epitaph that Apollinaire had written:

> *Hear us, kindly Rousseau.*
> *We greet you,*
> *Delaunay, his wife, Monsieur Quéval and I.*
> *Let our baggage through the Customs to the sky,*
> *We bring you canvas, brush and paint of ours,*
> *During eternal leisure, radiant*
> *As you once drew my portrait you shall paint*
> *The face of stars.*

> (Translated by Bertha Ten Eyck James)

DANIEL CATTON RICH

Film on Rousseau

VIOLON D'INGRES. Produced by Les Artisans d'Art du Cinéma, directed by J. B. Brunius and Georges Labrousse. 1939.

Circulated as *Hobbies Across the Sea* by the Museum of Modern Art Film Library. "It shows how the pastimes of laymen have provided some of the most famous works of modern art. The camera surveys works by the customs official Rousseau . . . and other self-taught artists."

One-man Exhibitions of Rousseau's Work

1910 NEW YORK, 291 Fifth Avenue (Alfred Stieglitz Gallery)—November 18 to December 8. Paintings and drawings belonging to Max Weber.

1911 PARIS, Quai d'Orsay (Pont de l'Alma), 29th Salon de la Société des Artistes Indépendants — April 20 to June 13 (extended to June 30). One gallery devoted to Rousseau.

1912 PARIS, Galerie Bernheim Jeune—December 25 to January 11, 1913. 50 paintings and drawings.

1923 PARIS, Galerie Paul Rosenberg—June.

1925 PARIS, Grande Maison de Blanc—October.

1926 BERLIN, Galerie Flechtheim — March. 32 paintings.

1926 LONDON, Lefèvre Gallery. October.

1931 NEW YORK, Marie Harriman Gallery—January 2 to February 12. 31 paintings.

Four new paintings exhibited October 29 to November 14.

1931 CHICAGO, Arts Club—February 20 to March 1. 7 paintings.

1933 BASEL, Kunsthalle—March 1 to April 2. 56 paintings, 8 drawings.

1937 PARIS, Galerie Paul Rosenberg—March 3–31. 22 paintings.

1942 CHICAGO, Art Institute—January 22 to February 23. 43 paintings.

Also exhibited at the Museum of Modern Art, New York, March 18 to May 3.

1944 PARIS, Musée d'Art Moderne—December 22, –45 1944 to January 21, 1945. 21 paintings.

1945 PARIS, Palais de Tokio, 56th Salon des Indépendents—March 2 to April 2. One memorial gallery devoted to Rousseau.

Bibliography

The arrangement is alphabetical, under the author's name, or under the title in the case of unsigned articles. Publications of museums are entered under the name of the city in which the museum is located. Exhibition catalogs issued by private galleries are listed under the name of the gallery.

Not included are references to some exhibition notes cited in the Art Index, to a few unillustrated exhibition catalogs, and to some articles mentioned in Huyghe (bibl.79), Grohmann (bibl.74) and Courthion (bibl.40).

This revised bibliography supplements and enlarges the list prepared in 1942 by the Art Institute of Chicago (bibl.121).

BERNARD KARPEL.

ABBREVIATIONS: Ap April, Ag August, Aufl edition, bibl. bibliography, c copyright, D December, ed editor, edition, F February, hft Heft, Ja January, Je June, Jl July, Mr March, My May, N November, no nr number, O October, p page(s), S September.

SAMPLE ENTRY for magazine article: RAYNAL, MAURICE. Le "banquet" Rousseau. Les Soirées de Paris 3no20:69–72 Ja 15 1913. EXPLANATION: An article entitled "Le 'banquet' Rousseau," by Maurice Raynal, will be found in Les Soirées de Paris, volume 3, number 20, pages 69 through 72 inclusive, January 15, 1913.

Writings by Rousseau

1 *Autobiographie d'Henri Rousseau*. Rédigée pour figurer dans le second tome de Portraits du prochain siècle (Girard-Coutance [sic] 1894) In Paris. Musée d'Art Moderne. Henri Rousseau (bibl.111).

First published by Soupault (bibl.139), reprinted by Wilenski (bibl.165). Rousseau's own account of his career up to July 10, 1895.

2 *L'Etudiant en Goguette*. In collaboration with Victor Louis Rivière. Comedy in 2 acts, 3 scenes. Date unknown.

An unpublished manuscript in the possession of Richard Aberle Florsheim, Chicago. The title page is apparently in Rousseau's handwriting, the text is in another hand. Nothing is known of the collaborator.

3 *La Vengeance d'une Orpheline Russe*. In collaboration with Mme. Barkowsky. Drama in 5 acts, 19 scenes. Date unknown.

Printed in full in Orbes no2 spring 1929; no3:101–6 spring 1932; no4:49–57 winter 1932–3. Excerpts in Flechtheim (bibl.59) and in Wilenski (bibl.165). Mentions Yadwigha as one of the characters, contains another character named Henri, and has considerable material on the glories and horrors of war. Nothing is known of the collaborator.

4 *Un Voyage à l'Exposition de 1889.* Vaudeville in 3 acts, 10 scenes. Date unknown, probably soon after 1889.

Excerpts printed in Le Bulletin de la Vie Artistique, 3no8:181–4 Ap 15 1922; no9:206–9 My 1 1922. From the manuscript in the possession of Robert Delaunay.

5 [Fac similé d'une lettre addressée a M. Ambroise-Vollard . . . 5/3 1910]

Reproduced in Paris. Musée d'Art Moderne. Henri Rousseau (bibl.111).

6 [Letters by Henri Rousseau] Les Soirées de Paris. 3no20:30–64 Ja 15 1913.

Important letters to Guillaume Apollinaire and others. Other letters in Soupault (bibl.139), Goldwater (bibl.68), Westheim (bibl.163).

7 [Poems by Henri Rousseau] Les Soirées de Paris. 3no20:65 Ja 15 1913.

8 [Three documents by Henri Rousseau] 1909?

In possession of Pierre Berès, New York. Receipts for money from Vollard for paintings furnished in 1909. "Rousseau also mentions the success his work has met in Russia and how pleased he is on this point" (from Berès letter, July 16, 1940, offering items for sale).

Literature on Rousseau

9 AJALBERT, JEAN. La leçon du Douanier. Beaux Arts p1,5 O 1 1937.

Reprints early criticism on Rousseau.

10 ALEXANDRE, ARSENE. [Notice on Rousseau] Comoedia Ap 3 1909.

10A America & Alfred Stieglitz, a collective portrait. Edited by Waldo Frank, Lewis Mumford, Dorothy Norman, Paul Rosenfeld & Harold Rugg. p109,239,314 Garden City, New York, Doubleday, Doran & Co., 1934.

11 APOLLINAIRE, GUILLAUME. The cubist painters, aesthetic meditations 1913. Translated from the French by Lionel Abel. p26–7 New York, Wittenborn and company, 1944.

Originally published as: Les peintres cubistes. Paris, Figuière, 1913.

12 —— Le Douanier. Les Soirées de Paris 3no20:7–29 Ja 15 1913.

13 —— Il y a. p17–19,97–100,146,152–78,192–3 Paris, Messein, 1925.

14 —— Souvenir du Douanier. *In* Paris. Musée d'Art Moderne. Henri Rousseau. p20–3 (bibl. 111).

"Ce poème a paru dans les Soirées de Paris, 13 août 1914."

15 ARP, HANS. Neue französiche Malerei. Eingeleitet von L. H. Neitzel. pl–2 Leipzig, Verlag der Weissen Bücher, 1913.

16 BASEL, KUNSTHALLE. Henri Rousseau. Kunsthalle Basel, 1. März bis 2. April 1933. 16p [Basel, 1933].

17 BASLER, ADOLPHE. Le "Douanier" Henri Rousseau. L'Art Vivant 2:777–9,782–3 O 1 1926.

18 —— Pariser chronik. Henri Rousseau bei Paul Rosenberg. Der Cicerone 15:839–40,843 S 1923.

19 —— Recollections of Henri Rousseau. The Arts 11:313–19 Je 1927.

20 —— Henri Rousseau (sa vie—son oeuvre). 52p Paris, Librairie de France [1927].

List of paintings, p4–6. Bibliography, p12. Also issued with imprint New York, Weyhe [1927].

21 —— Henri Rousseau. [11]p Paris, Gallimard, 1929. (Les peintres français nouveaux. no 34).

22 —— Henri Rousseau le Douanier. 4p plus 24 plates Paris, Librairie de France [1930?]. (Les albums d'art Druet. no 24).

BAZIN, GERMAIN. see bibl.80.

23 BELL, CLIVE. Since Cézanne. p49–56 New York, Harcourt, Brace, 1922.

Also in New Republic 18no232:335–6 Ap 12 1919.

24 BERTRAM, ANTHONY, ed. Henri Rousseau. [6]p plus 24 plates London, The Studio, 1936. (The world's masters. no18).

25 BOUCHER, LUCIEN. Le triomphe du Douanier Rousseau (dessins et photomontages). L'Art Vivant 1no24:38 D 15 1925.

25A BOURGEOIS, STEPHEN AND GEORGE, WALDEMAR. The French paintings of the XIXth and XXth centuries in the Adolph and Samuel Lewisohn collection. Formes no28–29:301,306 1932.

—— see also bibl.92.

26 BRAQUE, GEORGES, AND OTHERS. Testimony against Gertrude Stein. 15p The Hague, Servire Press, 1935.

Supplement to Transition no23 Jl 1935.

27 BULLIET, CLARENCE JOSEPH. The significant moderns and their pictures p64–70 New York, Covici-Friede, 1936.

28 BURGER, FRITZ. Cézanne und Hodler. Einführung in die Probleme der Gegenwart. 1:158–9 München, Delphin-Verlag, 1913.

28A BUZZICHINI, MARIO. Henri Rousseau. Milan, Ulrico Hoepli, 1944?

29 CANN, LOUISE GEBHARD. An artist of the "people." International Studio 31:251–6 Jl 1925.

29A CARCO, FRANCIS. Mémoires d'une autre vie. p402–3 Genève, Editions du Milieu du Monde, 1942.

30 CARY, ELIZABETH LUTHER. He saw no incongruity. New York Times p12 (section 8) Ja 4 1931.

Review of exhibition at Marie Harriman gallery.

30A CASTELFRANCO, GIORGIO. La pittura moderna. p44–7 Firenze, Luigi Gonelli, 1934.

31 CHASSÉ, CHARLES. Les fausses gloires; d'Ubu-Roi au Douanier Rousseau. La Grande Revue 111:177–212 Ap 1923.

32 ——Les défenseurs des fausses gloires; les amis du Douanier Rousseau. La Grande Revue 114:439–63 My 1924.

33 CHENEY, SHELDON. The story of modern art. p367–74 New York, Viking Press, 1941.

34 CHICAGO. ART INSTITUTE. Rousseau seminar under the auspices of the Scammon fund [2]p 1942.
   Program held February 4 in conjunction with the Rousseau exhibition.

35 CLARETIE, JULES. [Account of the Rousseau trial]. Figaro Ja 10 1909.

36 COCTEAU, JEAN. Cikánka Henri Rousseau. Volné Směry 25no2:35–6 1926.

36A COGNIAT, RAYMOND. Portraits of collectors: Jacques Doucet. Formes no2:11 F 1930.
   —— see also bibl.62.

36B COMBE, JACQUES. Un Douanier Rousseau au XVIIIe siècle: Frans Post (1612–1680). L'Amour de l'Art 12no12:481–9 D 1931.
   Includes stylistic and pictorial comparison with Rousseau.

37 COOPER, DOUGLAS. Henri Rousseau, artiste-peintre. Burlington Magazine 85:158,160–5 Jl 1944.

38 COQUIOT, GUSTAVE. Les indépendants, 1884–1920. p130–3,208 Paris, Ollendorff [1920].

39 —— Vagabondages à travers la peinture et les paysages, les bêtes et les hommes. 3.éd. p60–3 Paris, Ollendorff, 1921.

40 COURTHION, PIERRE. Henri Rousseau le Douanier. 51p plus 50 plates Genève, Editions d'Art Albert Skira, 1944.
   Supplement, p37–51, includes a chronology, list of dramatic works, exhibitions, and exhibited paintings, and a chronological bibliography.

41 —— Panorama de la peinture française contemporaine. 3.éd. p157–66 Paris, Simon Kra, 1927.

42 COUTURIER, M. A. The Douanier Rousseau [at the Museum of modern art] Commonweal 36no2:29–30 My 1 1942.

43 CROCKETT, JOHN. [Review of Henri Rousseau by Daniel Catton Rich] Harvard Advocate 129no1:28–30 S 1942.

44 CUNARD, NANCY. A recently discovered Rousseau. Horizon 11no66:407 Je 1945.

45 DAÜBLER, THEODOR. Henri Rousseau. Valori Plastici 2no9–12:98–100 1920.

46 DELAUNAY, ROBERT. Henri Rousseau le Douanier. L'Amour de l'Art 1no7:228–30 N 1920.

46A Dessins inédits de Rousseau. Cahiers d'Art no1:32–3 1927.

47 DORNAC, . . . [Deux portraits inédits d'Henri Rousseau]. L'Esprit Nouveau 2no14:163–5 1921.

48 DREYFUSS, ALBERT. Henri Rousseau le Douanier. Kunstchronik 25nr22:339–42 F 20 1914.

49 EBERLEIN, KURT KARL. Rousseau oder die Matrosen Kunst. Kunstchronik und Kunstmarkt 35nr48–9:721–4 Mr 6–13 1926.

50 EDDY, ARTHUR JEROME. Cubists and post-impressionism. p37 Chicago, McClurg, 1914.

50A EDOUARD-JOSEPH, RENÉ. Dictionnaire biographique des artistes contemporains, 1910–30. 3:235–6 Paris, Librairie Gründ, 1934.

51 EGGER, CARL. Der stil Henri Rousseaus; zur Erinnerung an die Ausstellung in der Basler Kunsthalle im März 1933. Basler Kunstverein Jahresbericht 1932. p3–16 [1933].

52 —— Henri Rousseau-Ausstellung in der Basler Kunsthalle. Die Kunst 67:225–9 My 1933.

53 EICHMANN, INGEBORG. Five sketches by Henri Rousseau. Burlington Magazine 72:300,302–3, 307 Je 1938.

54 EINSTEIN, CARL. Die Kunst des 20. Jahrhunderts. 2.Aufl. p47,238–48,558–9. Berlin, Propyläen-Verlag, 1928 [c1926]. (Propyläen Kunstgeschichte.XVI).

ELUARD, PAUL see bibl.111.

55 FELS, FLORENT. Le Douanier Rousseau. Nouvelles Littéraires, Artistiques et Scientifiques 4no157:4 O 17 1925.

56 —— Notes on the Rousseau exhibition at the Marie Harriman Gallery. Formes no11:10–12 Ja 1931.

56A —— Propos d'artistes. p144 Paris, La Renaissance du Livre, 1925.

57 FERNANDEZ, JUSTINO. Prometeo; ensayo sobre pintura contemporánea. p17–20. México, D. F., Porrua, 1945.

58 [FISCHKIN, ROSE MARY]. Cézanne, Rousseau, Chirico. Bulletin of the Art Institute of Chicago 20no5:62–4 My 1926.

59 FLECHTHEIM, ALFRED, GALERIE, BERLIN. Ausstellung Henri Rousseau. 39p 1926.
   Huyghe (bibl.79) refers to a Flechtheim catalog of the Rousseau exhibition at Dusseldorf, held March 1926, which contains articles by Uhde, Apollinaire, Siemsen, and excerpts from Rousseau's vaudeville.

59A FLORISOONE, MICHEL. A travers les expositions: Henri Rousseau [Galerie Rosenberg]. L'Amour de l'Art 18no3:97 Mr 1937.

60 GAUTHIER, MAXIMILIEN. La maison natale du Douanier Rousseau. Beaux Arts p1,3 D 3 1937.

61 ——— Henri Rousseau et Alfred Jarry seront célébrés à Laval, leur ville natale en juin prochain. Beaux Arts p1,5 F 11 1938.
——— see also bibl. 107, 111, 112.

62 GAZETTE DES BEAUX-ARTS, PARIS. Peintres instinctifs, naissance de l'expressionisme, décembre 1935–janvier 1936. Préface par André Salmon, catalogue par Raymond Cogniat. p[19–21] [1935]. (Les étapes de l'art contemporain.no15).
Nos. 120–136 are paintings by Rousseau.

63 GENAUER, EMILY. Notable exhibit [at the Museum of modern art] leaves Rousseau genius still an enigma. New York World Telegram Mr 21, 1942.

63A GEORGE, WALDEMAR. La grande peinture contemporaine à la collection Paul Guillaume. p55–60 Paris, Editions des Arts à Paris [192?].
Extract, with text in English and French, published in La Renaissance 12no4:172–85 Ap 1929.

64 ——— Le miracle de Rousseau. Les Arts à Paris no18:3–11 Jl 1 1931.
——— see also 25A.

65 GEORGES-MICHEL, MICHEL. Les grandes époques de la peinture "moderne" de Delacroix à nos jours. p121–3 New York-Paris, Brentano's, 1945.

66 ——— Peintres et sculpteurs que j'ai connus, 1900–1942. p100–2 New York, Brentano's, 1942.

GIRARD-COUTANCES see bibl.1.

67 GOLDWATER, ROBERT J. Primitivism in modern painting. New York & London, Harper & Brothers, 1938.
The modern primitives, p143–52. Bibliography, p208–9.

68 ——— & TREVES, MARCO. Artists on art. p404 New York, Pantheon Books, 1945.
Rousseau's letter to André Dupont dated April 1, 1910.

69 GORDON, JAN. Modern French painters. p65, 89,91–8,122,164,171 New York, Dodd, Mead, 1923.

70 GREY, ROCH. Souvenir de Rousseau. Les Soirées de Paris 3no20:66–8 Ja 15 1913.

71 ——— Henri Rousseau. Préface d'André Salmon. 53p plus 132 plates (4col) Paris, Galerie René Drouin [et] Editions "Tel," 1943.

72 ——— Henri Rousseau. 29p Rome, Editions de "Valori Plastici," 1922.
In French. Edition with English text, 1924. Originally published in Action 2no7:1–12 My 1921.

73 GRIOT, ALFRED. The centenary of Henri Rousseau. Art Quarterly 7no3:206–18 1944.

74 GROHMANN, WILL. Henri Rousseau. In U. Thieme & F. Becker, eds. Allegemeines lexikon der bildenden Künstler 29:113 Leipzig, Seemann, 1935.
Includes bibliography.

74A GUENNE, JACQUES. La naïveté est-elle un art? L'Art Vivant no147:140 Ap 1931.

75 HARRIMAN, MARIE, GALLERY, NEW YORK. Exhibition Henri Rousseau. 12p [1931].

76 HARTLEY, MARSDEN. Adventures in the arts. p144–54 New York, Boni and Liveright, 1921.

77 Henri Rousseau exhibition. Bulletin of the Art Institute of Chicago 36:17–20 F 1942.

78 HILDEBRANDT, HANS. Die Kunst des 19. und 20. Jahrhunderts. p361–3 Wildpark-Potsdam, Akademische Verlagsgesellschaft Athenaion, 1924 [postscript 1931].

79 HUYGHE, RENÉ. La peinture d'instinct; introduction. In R. Huyghe, ed. Histoire de l'art contemporain; la peinture. p185–8 Paris, Alcan, 1935.
Bibliography, p195–6. Originally published in L'Amour de l'Art no8:185–8,195–6 O 1933.

80 ——— La peinture française: les contemporains. Paris, P. Tisné, 1939.
Peinture populaire, p40–1. Notice biographique par Germain Bazin. Also issued in English edition by French and European Publications, New York.

80A L'Ingenuitat del pintor burot Henri Rousseau. Rivista Nova Ap 25 1914.
Reference from Courthion (bibl.40).

81 JACOMETTI, NESTO. Henri Rousseau dit le "Douanier." Le Point 2no3:87–8 1937.
JAKOVSKY, ANATOLE. See bibl.111.

82 JANIS, SIDNEY. Daniel Catton Rich, Henri Rousseau [a review]. College Art Journal 1no4:111–2 My 1942.

83 JEAN, RENÉ. Exposition Henri Rousseau (Galerie Bernheim). La Chronique des Arts no34: 273 N 16 1912.

83A ——— Expositions: Mathilde Seé, Francois-Charles Cachoud, Henri Rousseau (Galerie Georges Petit). La Chronique des Arts no6:44 F 11 1911.

84 KATZ, LEO. Understanding art. 2:338–42 [Chicago] Delphian Society, [reprint] 1940.

85 KIENITZ, JOHN FABIAN. Henri Rousseau. Art in America 30:122–5 Ap 1942.

86 KIESER, R. Henri Rousseau. Kunst und Künstler 11no4:218–20 Ja 1913.

87 KOLLE, HELMUD. Henri Rousseau. 15p Leipzig, Klinkhardt & Biermann, 1922. (Junge kunst. 27).
Text first published in Jahrbuch der Jungen Kunst p201–12 1921, and in Der Cicerone 13:371–82 Jy 1921.

87A Küppers, Paul Erich. Die Sammlung Max Leon Flemming in Hamburg. Der Cicerone 14hft 1:9 Ja 1922.

88 Larrabee, Ankey. Rousseau's ark [a poem]. Accent 4no3:139 spring 1944.

89 Lemaitre, Georges. From cubism to surrealism in French literature. p54,69–70,75 Cambridge, Mass., Harvard University Press, 1941.

90 Lhote, André. Exposition Henri Rousseau. Nouvelle Revue Française 21:627–9 N 1 1923.

91 ——— L'art populaire. Nouvelle Revue Française 16:274–6 Ag 1 1929.

92 Lewisohn, Adolph. The Adolph Lewisohn collection of modern French paintings and sculpture, with an essay on French painting during the nineteenth century and notes on each artist's life and works by Stephen Bourgeois. p8,189–97 New York, E. Weyhe, 1928.

93 Lewisohn, Samuel A. Painters and personality. p88–93 New York, Harper & Brothers, 1937.

94 Madsen, Hermann. Fran symbolism till surrealism. Stockholm, Ahlén & Söners Forlag, 1939.
Naivismen, p144–55.

95 M'Ahesa, Sent. Der Bräutigam Henri Rousseau. Der Querschnitt 10no8:514–6 Ag 1930.

96 McBride, Henry. Rousseau le Douanier. Art and Understanding 1:227–9 1930.

97 ——— The Rousseau show [at the Museum of modern art] New York Sun Mr 20 1942.

98 McCausland, Elizabeth. Henri Rousseau, dean of self-taught painters. Springfield Sunday Union and Republican (Mass.) Mr 29 1942.
Review of exhibition at the Museum of Modern Art.

99 Melville, Robert. Rousseau and Chirico. Scottish Art and Letters no1:31–5 1944.

100 Michailow, Nikola. Zur Begriffsbestimmung der Laienmalerei. Zeitschrift für Kunstgeschichte 4no5–6:283–300 1935.

100AMille, Pierre. Le peintre Henri Rousseau. Le Temps Ja 20 1913.
Reference from Courthion (bibl.40).

100BMilliken, William Mathewson. A painting by "Papa" Rousseau. Bulletin of the Cleveland Museum of Art 17no1:8–10 Ja 1930.

101 Mobius, M. R. Henri Rousseau—zum Selbstbildnis von 1890. Der Cicerone 18hft6:179–93 1926.

102 Moscow. Gosudarstvennyi Musei Novovo Zapadnovo Iskusstva. Thirty-five selected masterpieces from the Museum of western art in Moscow. plate 22(text) New York, New York Graphic Society [1936].
Text in Russian by Boris N. Ternovetz; captions in Russian and French.

102ANebbia, Ugo. Sul movimento pittorico contemporaneo. Emporium 38no228:428,432–3 D 1913.

102BNecrologie: [Henri Rousseau]. La Chronique des Arts no29:238 Ag 27 1910.

103 Nibbi, Gino. Rousseau le Douanier. Angry Penguins no4:17–19 1944.
"Translated from the Italian."

104 Niehaus, Kaspar. Henri Rousseau. Elsevier's Geïllustreerd Maandschrift 45:361–78 My 1913.

105 ——— Henri-Julien Rousseau. Elsevier's Geïllustreerd Maandschrift 42:297–305, 378–87 N–D 1932.

106 ——— Gauguin en Rousseau. (Coll. H. S.) Amsterdam, 1928.
Publication cited by Huyghe (bibl.79) and Grohman (bibl.74).

107 New York. Museum of Modern Art. Masters of popular painting; modern primitives of Europe and America. In collaboration with the Grenoble museum. Text by Holger Cahill, Maximilien Gauthier, Jean Cassou, Dorothy C. Miller and others. New York, 1938.
European section of modern primitives organized largely by Andry-Farcy of the Grenoble museum whose exhibit *Les Maîtres Populaires de la Réalité* was also shown, with modifications, in Zurich, 1937 and London, 1938. *Henri Rousseau* by Maximilien Gauthier, p39–43. Bibliography, p50–1.

107ANew York. Museum of Modern Art. Picasso: 50 years of his art. By Alfred H. Barr, Jr. p59,265–6 New York, 1946.

——— see also bibl.121.

108 Nezval, Vítězslav. Henri Rousseau. 4p plus 25 plates V Praze, Melantrich a.s., 1937. (Prameny, sbírko dobrého umění. Svazek 14).

109 O'Connor, John, Jr. Henri Rousseau. Exhibition of paintings at the Carnegie Institute from December 4 to December 27. Carnegie Magazine 16:209–13 D 1942.

110 Olivier, Fernande. Picasso et ses amis. p76–83,110–13 Paris, Stock, 1933. (Collection "Ateliers." 4).
Extracts published as *Among the artists of the modern movement* London Studio 7no37:200 Ap 1934.

111 Paris. Musée d'Art Moderne de la Ville de Paris. Henri Rousseau, le Douanier. Exposition organisée par le Front national des arts pour commémorer le centenaire de la nais-

sance de Henri Rousseau, 22 décembre–21 janvier 1945. [Paris, 1944].

Contents: *Henri Rousseau le Douanier*, Paul Eluard.—*Autobiographie d'Henri Rousseau*.—*Gentil Rousseau*, Anatole Jakovsky.—*Fac similé d'une lettre addressée a M. Ambroise-Vollard*.—*Souvenir du Douanier*, Guillaume Apollinaire.—*Les amis d'Henri Rousseau*, Maximilien Gauthier.—*Catalogue*.

112 PARIS. MUSÉE DE GRENOBLE. Les maîtres populaires de la réalité. Avant-propos de Raymond Escholier, textes et notices de Maximilien Gauthier. Exposition organisé à Paris par le Musée de Grenoble. 72p plus 44 plates 1937.

113 PAYRÓ, JULIO E. Rousseau el Aduanero. 72p Buenos Aires, Editorial Poseidon, 1944.

114 PEVSNER, NIKOLAUS. Pioneers of the modern movement from William Morris to Walter Gropius. p83–6 London, Faber & Faber, 1936.

115 QUIGLEY, JANE. Henri Rousseau: Douanier. Artwork 3no12:250–4 Ja–Mr 1928.

116 RAYNAL, MAURICE. Le "banquet" Rousseau. Les Soirées de Paris 3no20:69–72 Ja 15 1913.

117 —— Picasso. p52–60 München, Delphin Verlag, 1921.

118 —— Picasso. p44–52 Paris, Crès, 1922.

119 —— Le salon des indépendants. L'Esprit Nouveau 2no14:1636–8 1921.

120 READ, HERBERT. Henri Rousseau. Now 3:30–2 1945.

121 RICH, DANIEL CATTON. Henri Rousseau. 80p New York, Museum of Modern Art, 1942.

Monograph issued "in collaboration with the Art Institute of Chicago" for a joint exhibition. Includes annotated bibliography.

122 RICHTER, IRMA ANNA. Henri Rousseau exhibition [at the Museum of modern art]. College Art Journal 1no4:107–8 My 1942.

123 ROH, FRANZ. Ein neuer Henri Rousseau; zur kunstgeschichtlichen Stellung des Meisters. Der Cicerone 16:710–6 Jl 1924.

Also published in Jahrbuch der Jungen Kunst p57–60 1924.

123A —— Nach-expressionismus, magischer Realismus. p80–1,123–4 Leipzig, Klinghardt u. Biermann, 1925.

124 —— Zum Begriff der Laienkunst; Malereien eines Matrosen. Der Cicerone 17:470–1,473–5 My 1925.

125 —— Henri Rousseaus Bildform und Bedeutung für die Gegenwart. Die Kunst 55:105–14 Ja 1927.

Also published in Die Kunst für Alle 42:104–14 1927.

126 ROSENBERG, PAUL, GALERIE, PARIS. Exposition Henri Rousseau (1844–1910) du mercredi 3 mars au mercredi 31 mars 1937. [12]p [1937].

127 [ROUSSEAU, HENRI]. Dodici opere di Rousseau. 2p plus 12 plates Firenze, Libreria della Voce, 1914. (Maestri moderni. 2).

128 Rousseau — primitive or professional? Art News 41:18–20 F 15 1942.

129 Rousseau: no primitive, no douanier. Art News 41:25 Ap 1 1942.

130 SALMON, ANDRÉ. Propos d'atelier. p137–48 Paris, Crès, 1922.

130A —— Henri Rousseau dit le Douanier. Vell I Nou 2no16:120–4 Jl 1921.

131 —— Henri Rousseau dit le Douanier. 140p Paris, Crés, 1927. (Peintres et sculpteurs).

131A —— Le tombeau d'Henri Rousseau. Action 2no10:10–12 N 1921.

132 —— Vstup celniká Rousseaua do Louvru. Volné Směry 24no3–4:90–1 1925–6.

Also published in L'Art Vivant 1no21:29–30 N 1 1925.

—— see also bibl.62,71.

132A SAN LAZZARO, G. DI. Cinquant' anni di pittura moderna in Francia. p91–3 Roma, Stablimenti Danesi, 1945.

133 SARDE, JACQUES. Henri Rousseau. Pour La Victoire Ap 25 1942.

Newspaper account of exhibition at the Museum of Modern Art.

134 SCHEFFLER, KARL. Henri Rousseau. Kunst und Künstler 24hft7:290,292 Ap 1926.

Exhibition at Flechtheim gallery.

135 SOFFICI, ARDENGO. Henry [sic] Rousseau. La Voce 2no40:395–6 S 15 1910.

136 —— La France jugée à l'étranger; le peintre Henry [sic] Rousseau. Mercure de France 87:748–55 O 1910.

Translation of bibl. 135, with a prefatory note by Lucile Dubois.

137 LES SOIRÉES DE PARIS. No. 20 consacré au peintre Henri Rousseau le Douanier. 72p Ja 15 1913.

For contents see bibl.6,7,12,70,116.

138 SOUPAULT, PHILIPPE. La légende du Douanier Rousseau. L'Amour de l'Art 7no10:333–7 O 1926.

139 —— Henri Rousseau, le Douanier. 59p Paris, Editions des Quatre Chemins, [1927].

Contains Rousseau's autobiographical note and letters.

140 STEIN, GERTRUDE. The autobiography of Alice B. Toklas. p126–32 New York, Harcourt, Brace, 1933.

141 SULZER, EVA. Did Henri Rousseau ever get to Mexico? Dyn 2:26–7 Jl–Ag 1942.

142 SWEENEY, JAMES JOHNSON. Henri Rousseau exhibition [at the Museum of modern art]. College Art Journal 1no4:108–10 My 1942.

143 ———— Plastic redirections in twentieth century painting. p15 Chicago, University of Chicago Press, 1934.

144 SZITTYA, EMIL. Henri Rousseau. Hamburg, Asmus Verlag, 1924.
Publication cited by Huyghe (bibl.79).

145 ———— Malerschicksale: vierzehn porträts. Hamburg, Asmus Verlag, 1925?
Essays on Rousseau, Van Gogh, Chagall and others.

TERNOVETZ, BORIS, N. see bibl.102.

THIEME & BECKER. see bibl.74.

146 TOOTH, ARTHUR AND SONS, LONDON. Les maîtres populaires de la réalité. February 17–March 12. 32p [London, 1938].
Catalog of an exhibition held previously in Paris and Zurich, 1937.

147 TROHEL, JULES. Origines mayennaises du Douanier Rousseau. Mercure de France 205: 710–14 Ag 1 1928.

148 UHDE, WILHELM. Henri Rousseau. 66p Paris, Figuière, 1911.

149 ———— Henri Rousseau; herausgegeben durch die Galerie Alfred Flechtheim, Düsseldorf. 67p Düsseldorf, Ohle, 1914.
First German edition.

150 ———— An Henri Rousseau. Genius 1:190–3 1919.

151 ———— Henri Rousseau. Deutsche Kunst und Dekoration 47:16–26 O–N 1920.

152 ———— Henri Rousseau. 89p Dresden, Kaemmerer, 1921. (Künstler der Gegenwart. band 2).
Revised German edition of Uhde's 1911 book with fewer and different plates and some additional text.

153 ———— Henri Rousseau. 2.Aufl. 89p Berlin & Dresden, Kaemmerer, 1923. (Künstler der Gegenwart).

154 ———— Picasso and the French tradition. p41–6 Paris, Editions des Quatre Chemins; New York, Weyhe, 1929.
Originally published as: Picasso et la tradition française. Paris, Editions des Quatre Chemins, 1928.

155 ———— Henri Rousseau et les primitifs modernes. In R. Huyghe, ed. Historie de l'art contemporain; la peinture p189–96 Paris, Alcan, 1935.
Originally published in L'Amour de l'Art no8:189–96 O 1933.

156 ———— Von Bismarck bis Picasso; Erinnerungen und Bekenntnisse. p150–2,156–8,247–54 Zürich, Oprecht, 1938.

156A VALENTINER, WILHELM R. Expressionism and abstract painting. Art Quarterly 4no3:214 summer 1941.

157 VANITY FAIR'S PORTFOLIO OF MODERN FRENCH ART. With biographical and critical notes on 31 masters and an introduction by R. H. Wilenski. p[9], plate 19(text) New York, Vanity Fair, 1935.

158 VAUDOYER, JEAN-LOUIS. Trente ans d'art libre. A propos de la retrospective des "Indépendants." Revue de l'Art Ancien et Moderne 49:226–36 Ap 1926.

158A VLAMINCK, MAURICE DE. Aus Vlamincks memoiren. Die Kunst 61no7:208,211 Ap 1930.

159 VOLLARD, AMBROISE. Recollections of a picture dealer. p93–4,196,215–9 London, Constable, 1936.
Translated by Violet M. MacDonald. Also issued with imprint Boston, Little, Brown, 1936.

160 WARNOD, ANDRÉ. Les berceaux de la jeune peinture: Montmartre, Montparnasse. p50,84, 185,230 Paris, Michel, 1925.

WARTMANN, W. see bibl.169.

160A WATT, ALEXANDER. Notes from Paris. Apollo 23no134:108 F 1936.
Review of exhibition Peintres Instinctifs (bibl.62).

161 WEBER, MAX. Rousseau as I knew him. Art News 41:17,35 F 15 1942.

162 WELLINGTON, H. Rousseau, le Douanier. 137: 673–4 Spectator O 23 1926.

163 WESTHEIM, PAUL, ed. Künstler Bekenntnisse: Briefe, Tagebuchblätter, Betrachtungen heutiger Künstler. p133–9 Berlin, Propyläen-Verlag [1923].

164 WILENSKI, REGINALD HOWARD. French painting p327–9 Boston, Hale, Cushman & Flint, 1931.

165 ———— Modern French painters. p80–2,119–20, 134–5, 181–3, 205–7, 243–7, 360–3, 372–7, and passim New York, Reynal & Hitchcock, 1940.
The most complete account of Rousseau's career and art. Bibliography, p360–1.
———— see also bibl.157.

166 ZERVOS, CHRISTIAN. Henri Rousseau et le sentiment poétique. Cahiers d'Art 1no9:227–36 1926.

167 ———— Rousseau. 96p Paris, Editions Cahiers d'Art, 1927. (Les grands peintres d'aujourd'hui. no2).

168 ———— Histoire de l'art contemporain. p99–112 Paris, Editions Cahiers d'Art, 1938.

169 ZÜRICH. KUNSTHAUS. Les maîtres populaires de la réalité. p11–12,17–19 1937.
Exhibition catalog. Text by W. Wartmann.

This reprinted edition was produced by the offset printing process. The text and plates
were photographed separately from the original volume, and the plates rescreened. The
paper and binding were selected to ensure the long life of this library grade edition.

*Nine thousand five hundred copies of this second revised edition have been printed in May 1946 for the
Trustees of the Museum of Modern Art by The John B. Watkins Company, New York. The color plates were
printed by Wm. E. Rudge's Sons, New York.*

Rousseau

Henri Rousseau
peintre.
~~~

Né à Laval en l'année 1844, vu le manque de
fortune de ses parents, fut obligé de suivre
tout d'abord une autre carrière que celle ou
ses goûts artistiques l'appelaient.

Ce ne fut donc qu'en l'année 1885
qu'il fit ses débuts dans l'art après bien des
déboires, seul sans autre maître que la
nature, et quelques conseils reçus de Gérôme
et de Clément. Ses deux premières créations
exposées furent envoyées au Salon des Champs
Elysées, elles avaient pour titre Une danse
Italienne et un Coucher de soleil. L'année
suivante il créa de nouveau Un soir de
Carnaval, un coup de tonnerre. Puis ensuite
Dans l'attente, un pauvre Diable, Après
le Festin, Le Départ, Dîner sur l'herbe.